It Doesn't Take a Village

It Doesn't Take a Village

by
Stephen P. Dixon, Ph.D.

CeShore

Pittsburgh, PA

ISBN 1-58501-014-6

Trade Paperback
© Copyright 2000 Stephen Dixon
All rights reserved
First Printing—2000
Library of Congress #99-64524

Request for information should be addressed to:

CeShore Publishing Company
The Sterling Building
440 Friday Road
Pittsburgh, PA 15209
www.ceshore.com

Cover Design: Michelle S. Vennare - SterlingHouse Publisher
Art: Michelle Vennare - SterlingHouse Publisher
Typesetting: McBeth Typesetting and Design
CeShore is an imprint of SterlingHouse Publisher, Inc.

Printed in Canada

TABLE OF CONTENTS

DEDICATION

I dedicate this book to the parents who struggle with the arduous task of child rearing. They understand the frustration of trying to teach their kids valuable lessons while allowing them to be themselves and learn sometimes by failing. To my parents who were successful at their parenting as they raised eight kids to adulthood. To my wife and kids. It is through them that I am able to stay focused on the important things in life. Nothing is more important than bringing children into the world. My wife and I are responsible with giving our children the necessary tools, teaching them the lessons, and loving them unconditionally so that they may one day bring their own children into this world. This divine perpetuation has no equal.

Finally, to my sister Mary. God did not give her children of her own before she passed on in 1993, but instead He made her so special that she inspired everyone she crossed paths with. I am thankful that she was a part of my life, and, I am even more thankful that my daughters knew her. I know that she is watching over us.

PROLOGUE

Over the last five decades a plethora of books have been written to help parents gain a better understanding of their children.

I am a clinical psychologist and father of four. I received my formal graduate training at Georgia State University, where I enrolled in the Family and Child Clinical Track. I have been working with adolescents and their families for over ten years. In that time I have run parenting groups on adolescent psychiatric inpatient units, treated families with child rearing problems in outpatient settings, and given hundreds of seminars on parenting. Much of this book will address the common problems and concerns that parents approach me with as they attempt to successfully parent their children.

Parents begin encountering new behaviors and difficulties when their children are between the ages of nine and eighteen. Teaching children personal responsibility can be a very difficult task. This book can help parents with this task. Even though many of the examples you will read about describe children in the pre-adolescent (i.e., nine to thirteen) and adolescent stages (i.e., thirteen to eighteen) of development, the parenting philosophy expounded on here applies to children of all ages. This book has been stirring in my mind for nearly three years now, and it is time that I put my thoughts to paper. I sincerely hope that the finished product is helpful for you.

Parents today are feeling more helpless and powerless than ever before. The parenting issues they face on a daily basis keep them hopping: their kids are getting suspended from school, or are running away from home, some are getting into juvenile gangs and involving themselves in criminal behavior, and some are experimenting with drugs and sexually acting out. Parents experience their children being disrespectful at home, and their children refuse to respond to any structure or limits imposed on them. Today's parents are frustrated and they feel a lack of support from the community in which they live. Many parents even believe that community services and agents are working against them. I have talked to parents who are frustrated with school systems, court systems, and social service agencies in their towns. For example, parents can not believe that schools would allow, and in some cases encourage, kids sixteen years of age and older to drop out. Parents who deal with social service agencies become angry when they are accused of abusive or neglectful parenting because they have exercised the same type of discipline that their parents exercised on them. Rather than help the struggling family, the social service worker is looked upon as an intrusion or invasion by parents who encounter the department's visit. Another example of parental frustration with the established systems centers around the local police departments. Parents have a hard time with local police departments that tell them that they can do nothing when their child has run away or worse, when their fourteen year old daughter is active sexually with eighteen and nineteen year old boys. Finally, parents are frustrated at some of the laws that have passed that supposedly protect the child. Most parents can not believe that fourteen and fifteen year old children can seek out services without their knowledge or consent. They get angry when they find out that their kids are experimenting with lethal recreational drugs, or have sought out birth control or abortion services. When parents discover that the professionals who have treated their child can not breach the child's confidentiality and inform them, they often feel undermined and sabotaged in their child rearing task. In short, today's parents feel that their job is hard enough, and further believe that in many cases society is working against them.

Parents look to their own adolescence as the major frame of reference in trying to understand their own teenagers. Although the physical, emotional, and cognitive developmental stage we call adolescence has not changed much in the last generation or two, the society that we live in has made major changes. Parents can understand and accept that their teenager is striving for independence and autonomy. They can also understand and accept that peers have taken on significant importance. Most parents can even understand that questioning of authority and feelings of invincibility characterize their adolescent. These things were true when they were teenagers, and as such they are easily recognized and understood when they are displayed by their own kids. Today's parents, however, often neglect to consider the major societal changes that have occurred since they were in adolescence. The changes that have occurred in our society have influenced the behaviors of our youth.

A generation ago, adolescents were not bringing handguns and knives to school. A generation ago, teenagers were not driving by in cars and shooting at other people. Teenage girls did not view sexual behavior in casual ways, or pursue boys with the vigor and obviousness that we see today. Virginity was a virtue for young women a generation ago; today it is a slight. Even though the generation of the 1960's touted free love and drugs, the reality is that sexual freedom and drug use did not occur among our thirteen to seventeen year old children. Rather, it occurred on college campuses across America. High schools were free of the "free love" notion that characterized the sexual revolution of the 1960's and early 1970's. If you doubt this, ask yourself: would your mom or dad have been okay with you carrying a condom around just in case you happened upon a sexual encounter when you were fourteen? In many of our high schools today, kids receive free condoms to protect themselves from the consequences of sex. AIDS and other sexually transmitted diseases have become so dangerous that our educational institutions have taken charge of the issue. The societal attitude around teenage sex has shifted from "Teach your children to wait until adulthood and marriage to engage in sexual intercourse" to "You know kids are going to have sex - there is no stopping that fact, so let us at least teach them about safe sex." Along with this attitude of hopelessness, paradoxically, has come a great deal of hope. We have begun to *hope* that our normally irresponsible teenager will engage in responsible sexual behavior! This promiscuous societal attitude is not consistent with the view of sex that most parents have about their own teens, but it reflects the more liberal views of our educators, the national media, our policy makers, and our politicians.

Drug use has evolved a generation as well. It is true that today's parents are not strangers to illicit drug use. Marijuana, acid, and other substances were around a generation ago. Twenty five years ago, however, it was more of a fringe element of adolescence (i.e., some teens engaged; most did not). Today, drug use has evolved and peer pressure around "getting high" has emerged. Not every teen today is engaging in drug use, but clearly the acceptance of it is prevalent in our high schools and middle schools; that is, most of the kids who choose not to engage in recreational drug use are not very critical of their peers who do. There are also new drugs out there today that were not around a generation ago. Designer drugs such as pot laced with PCP, rocks of crack cocaine, and crystal methamphetamine "speed", have penetrated the schools that our children attend.

Another obvious societal change concerns the family. We all know that the family structure has changed, but, as with most changes, we do not know how it has contributed to the behaviors that we see in our children. A generation ago most families remained two-parent households. Divorce was rare, so single-parent and step-parent situations were also rare. Today, there are more single-parent households, more step-parenting situations and more homes with both parents employed full-time in the work force. Today's home simply looks much different than it looked twenty five to thirty years ago. I believe that one consequence of this change can be seen by one simple comparison: If you ask parents about their home situation when they were adolescents, most will say that they knew the rules and expectations of their home. Today's adolescent, however, is less sure. The rules, for whatever reasons, have not been clarified for him or her. When parents say that they understood the rules established by their parents, they are also saying that they understood the consequences for breaking those boundaries. **It is one of the tenets of this book that parents today do inform kids of their expectations and rules. The problems come when consequences and rewards are required.** Today's parents are having extreme difficulties juggling the demands of their world. Inconsistent parenting appears to be one of the prices that the home and the family has paid for the societal changes that have occurred in the last thirty years. One goal of this book is to put consistent parenting back into the home.

Not surprisingly, teenagers today report increased stresses and pressures in their lives. These pressures include those of yesteryear and more. Without the consistent structure and stability of yesteryear's family life, the adolescent today is engaging in more destructive behavior than ever before. Homicides and suicides among our youth have become so prevalent that our society has almost grown callous to them. One can hardly sit down to watch the evening news these days without hearing about some teenager's tragic and senseless death.

One of the reasons I wrote this book is to give parents a strategy and a philosophy to address today's youth. I want this book to help them provide the kind of structure at home that today's teenager requires. This book is for the single parent who often feels all alone in the parenting task, the step parent family who are struggling with new roles, and the "traditional" (i.e., natural mother and father) family. This book will identify the goals of parenting, and describe an effective way of reaching those goals. If you find yourself reading my suggestions for parental responses and saying, "I tried that," then you are not in the right frame of mind to make this work. My approach to parenting is not a "try"; it is a philosophy. If you are trial and error parents, your kids will know that your approach at any given time is fleeting. The kind of parenting described in this book is not a "try" it: rather, it is a "believe and do" approach.

It is important to spend some time examining and defining our parenting goals. If we were Bengal tigers instead of human beings, and we had a litter of cubs, what would our parenting tasks look like? When would those tasks end? What would our parenting goals be? For the Bengal tiger it is to raise the cub to a certain physical age and up to a skill level at which the cub could make it on his own. This includes making sure that the curious cub does not enter dangerous situations (i.e., playing near the king cobra), since the cub does not have the experience, judgment, or physical prowess to survive this situation. Bengal tigers know when their cubs are ready to leave home.

With our children, our society has said that age eighteen is the age when the child **can** leave home. The Bengal tiger does not have a set age; instead, the tiger displays a set of behaviors that tell the parent that the cub is ready to leave. It seems, then, that Bengal tigers teach their cubs certain tasks, and coach them in certain situations, and then they let them go. They move from protector and provider to teacher and coach. What things move the parent tiger to kick the cub (now a young tiger) out of the pride? First, the young tiger shows that it can make a kill. This tells the parents that the cub can feed himself. In the world of tigers this is quite a strong message. Parent tigers realize that the cub can make it on his own, and their instincts tell them that their young tiger will now compete for the same food that keeps them alive.

We are not Bengal tigers, but we can use strategies that are similar to theirs. We can identify behaviors and skills that we want our children to acquire during their childhood. We want to teach our children important survival lessons, and as involved parents we try to keep them away from danger. We try to help our children reach a point where they can survive the world without our supervision. We also want to give our kids certain tools. We give them the tools that have helped us make it. These tools round out their physical, emotional, and cognitive skills.

Let me give you an example, in relation to the comparison to the tiger parent that I talked about earlier. We want to teach our own young to stay away from drugs, since they can be as dangerous to them as the king cobra is to the tiger cub! We realize that at some point we can't really control our children's behavior, and we fear that our children may try to experiment with drugs and other dangerous things. One wonders if the Bengal tiger parent fears that at some point the young tiger will take on the cobra snake when the parent is not around.

It is clear that parenting is a complicated and complex task. Certainly there are many goals that we strive for as parents. Still, when broken down to the barest essentials, we hope to be successful tool givers for our kids. Parents strive to give children various tools by which to live their lives. Among these are **survival tools, value tools, tangible tools, and psychological tools**. By **survival tools** we mean the development of good judgment and decision-making skills The category called **value tools** include standards by which children should treat others, including standards of right and wrong, and the role of spirituality in their lives. The **tangible tools** refer to skills that help children seek a college education or trade skills with which they will be able to make a living and take care of themselves financially. **Psychological tools** are skills that help children learn about themselves and aid them in developing self-esteem.

Teaching our values and giving our children a strong sense of self-worth is a process that takes a long time. They learn these things by watching us and by participating in the experiences that make up their everyday lives. Children learn to care for themselves because they are cared for, and they gain self-worth by being recognized for the unique contributions that they bring to the world.

It Doesn't Take a Village focuses on teaching children about personal responsibility. We want our children to become the authors of their own thoughts and actions. We want them to learn to accept responsibility for their own choices and behaviors. **It Doesn't Take a Village** aids parents in this seemingly never-ending task.

In **It Doesn't Take a Village** you will learn how to become a more effective tool giver for your child. You will learn how your own emotional output often times interferes with this tool giving task. You will learn strategies for dealing with feelings of powerlessness, and you will learn ways of getting back in charge of your family and your home.

I realize that portions of this book may sound like descriptions of how to get the best of your enemy (i.e., how to win power struggles with your kids). Children are not our enemies, though, and power struggles usually benefit no one. This book is about dealing with difficult situations that arise. It is about establishing a parenting philosophy that reduces the chances that your family and your child will get into these difficult situations. I want to direct the reader back to our parenting goals, and constantly remind parents that they are tool givers for their children.

As you read this book, I want you to know that my descriptions of the children I have treated in my practice are more accurately descriptions of the parents that I have worked with. This book is not about the kids - it is about the parents. I will be addressing the difficulties of parenting and, admittedly, I will give little time to the parts of parenting that give us the most joy.

This book's focus is on how to parent children when struggles do occur. To be an effective parent, you must know the developmental issues that your child is struggling with. For example, in adolescence the drive for independence is second only to the drive for peer acceptance. This striving for independence is internal, and it sets up internal conflicts with authority figures and imposed limits. In chapters four, five, six, and seven you will receive information regarding your child's developmental stages. This information will help direct you toward appropriate and effective parental responses. When the book gives examples of parenting that deal with adolescence they may sound a lot like "How to win power struggles with your teen." On the contrary, **It Doesn't Take a Village** is a tool we can utilize to avoid the teenager-parent arguments.

We can start by acknowledging that parenting is damned hard, and that there is no such thing as a perfect parent. We as parents have made mistakes, and we will make more down the road. I do believe, however, that if you use **It Doesn't Take a Village** as your guide, your mistakes will not be as significant or severe, and, just as important, you will be able to rebound to effective teaching and coaching of your children.

As children grow up, they present different challenges for their parents. This book will help parents deal with the unique challenges they face from their kids. The parents who are dealing with a nine or ten year old who seems to need constant reminding in order to complete even the most simple requests, will get help from chapter four. The parents with an eleven or twelve year old who have witnessed the child's grades drop from A's and B's to near failing, will gain valuable information about why this occurs and what to do about it in chapter five. Do you have a thirteen or fourteen year old who presents as if they "know it all", in your home? Do they argue with you over nearly every request, every statement, every limit you impose? Is there a struggle over the friends they have chosen? **It Doesn't Take a Village** addresses these challenges too. And what about the challenges presented to the parents of older adolescents? Dating behavior, curfews, driving, experimentation with alcohol and drugs, and emancipation from home are all topics that you will find addressed in this book.

The result of successful parenting is the greatest reward of all. Reaching a successful result depends on how we define our relationship with our kids (i.e., how we provide, teach, and love our children). The result is less about how we deal with one or two difficult situations that arise in our parenting journey, and more about how we do overall in that journey. This book will help you as you continue on that ever important journey.

CHAPTER ONE

An Introduction to Unemotional Parenting

IN CHAPTER ONE YOU WILL FIND

- The effective parenting philosophy
- Things that frustrate parents
- Dealing with frustration by remembering the tools that we want to give our children
- Spanking and other corporal techniques of discipline

You might be wondering, "Can this guy be serious?" You might be thinking, "No one can be unemotional when they are dealing with their own kids." For many of us, the parenting relationship is the most important relationship in our lives. Sometimes it surpasses the marital relationship (i.e., you really can't divorce your kids). The minute your child is born an emotional bond is established. You are thrilled with your children's accomplishments, and disappointed with their failures. You teach and protect, you become important role models for them, and most importantly you love them. So what am I talking about? We can no sooner be unemotional where our kids are concerned than be eagles who are afraid of heights. It just is not in our nature.

Unemotional Parenting is not about caring less, and it is not about loving less. **Unemotional Parenting** is about being the most effective parent you can be. It is about teaching and it is about leading by example, two extremely important tasks that contribute to effective parenting.

Because we have such an emotional bond with our children, it is very difficult to respond to them without letting our emotional sides influence our response. When we are angry, frustrated, or just simply fatigued, these emotions can influence our behaviors toward our children. The philosophy and strategies contained in this book will help you set aside these negative emotions and become more effective in handling your kids.

When we respond to our kids in an emotional way, that is when we let our emotions influence our parenting decisions - often times we become less effective parents. This is a major theme that helps define the philosophy of **Unemotional Parenting.** Our children and their behaviors often frustrate us. The nine year old who almost never responds to mom's requests the first time she requests something causes frustration. The sixteen year old who frequently comes home after curfew or leaves the home without informing parents of his or her whereabouts and plans causes frustration. The twelve and thirteen year old siblings who seemingly fight over everything and require mom or dad to step in and referee the constant squabbles causes parental frustration and anger. The fourteen year old who ties up the telephone for hours after school, comes home with a poor report card then claims that she is trying as hard as she can causes frustration. These are just some common examples of how frustration gets going and causes emotional responses from parents. This book and the unemotional parenting philosophy will help reduce frustration, and it will give you ways to deal with the frustration and anger more effectively than you have in the past.

Remembering the role we maintain as parents and the overall goal of parenting helps us deal with the emotional side of parenting. The ultimate role we play with our children is the role of tool giver. As primary role models to our children we are constantly providing tools for them. They watch us deal with frustration and anger and they learn how to deal with frustrating things that occur in their lives through this observation. We contribute to their sense of self and their self esteem in the ways we show approval and disapproval. Children get a sense of fairness and justice first from their parents, and later from other experiences they experience outside of the home. Parents are the most important influence in children's lives. Effective and consistent parenting helps them become successful adults. Unemotional parenting will help parents give their children the tools they need.

Lets start with unemotional parenting by looking at a controversial issue in parenting: the issue of spanking and corporal punishment.

SPANKING, THE ULTIMATE EMOTIONAL RESPONSE

Frustrated parents today frequently recall the manner in which they were parented, and they attach strange loyalties to techniques that were neither effective nor appropriate. One of these techniques is spanking or hitting children when they get out of line. Yesterday's parents applied corporal punishment when their kids showed disrespect for them or their rules. Kids often feared their father and did things to avoid experiencing his wrath. Or did they? Let's look at why spanking is a poor parenting tool, and why I maintain that it always has been.

One great equalizer for kids in their struggles with their parents is getting the parent to respond emotionally. Spanking is more times than not the end result of a parent who is frustrated, angry, and emotional.

When a child is very young (i.e., two years old), and he or she is about to touch a hot burner on a stove, or play with an electric socket, the good parent may shout "NO" and paddle the child's diapered fanny in a firm (but not hard) way. The child, startled by the "NO" and by the spanking on the diaper, learns a very valuable lesson. The lesson he learns is not to go near the hot stove or outlet again. The parent in this situation is picking a strategy that is effective and appropriate. This is not a situation of parental anger or frustration, however. Even though the parent may have appropriately applied spanking to the two year old, the parent often feels badly because of it. In teaching the child a valuable lesson they have made him cry and sob. The sad child makes the parent feel bad, and the parent then often does something to make the child feel better again. A parent may hold the child close to them; they may softly explain to the virtually non-communicative toddler that they are not angry with them, and they may even offer a peace offering of a lollipop or a story. The parent often tries something to make up with the child, who was appropriately disciplined. This is human nature. Let's look at the spanking and the punishment, though: If done correctly, the "NO" serves as a strong punisher because it is paired with a spanking. The word "NO" comes to mean parental disapproval, and at ages two to eight disapproval is a strong reinforcer.

Let's look at the effectiveness of the physical part of the punishment, however. What happens as kids get older and bigger? They talk back, learn to openly defy their parents, and to test their parent's limits. The lessons we try to teach kids as they grow older change from "Don't touch that because it will hurt you" to "Do this or that because I told you to." The emphasis in teaching the older child, then, is teaching them to respect adults and to conform to rules. As kids get bigger, they require harder spankings. The parent must ask themselves, "Is the spanking a teaching tool, or is it a way I deal with my own anger and emotions?" As boys approach adolescence, they often develop different ways of viewing corporal discipline from adults. For example, when I was in the fifth grade, the principal at my school would paddle us when we were sent to his office for disciplinary reasons. I got two swats from him during that year, and I was in terror on both occasions. I cried like a baby with both swats, and I did not want to return to his office. A strange thing happened, however, between the fifth and sixth grades. I moved from fearing the principal's swats to almost seeking them out. A group of the sixth grade boys set up a "macho" contest to see who could get the most swats during the year. None of the participants cried after receiving a swat; we were getting big, and crying was for babies. As a group we all cheered on the bad actor after he got his swat from the principal. Peer opinion became very important to me during that year. Do you want to know how the principal responded? He began hitting harder. He was going to make sure that we felt it. He hated the notion that some twelve year old kid would get the best of him, but the harder he hit us, the more he fed into our machismo. Somewhere along the developmental road, that corporal punishment technique lost its effectiveness on the male students. We laughed knowing that we were actually getting the best of the disciplinarian, and that nothing he could do or was doing would hurt us. I got forty-nine swats from the principal in my sixth grade year. I finished third out of five in the group of trouble-makers.

At home the same is true. What at one time may have been effective (i.e., the two year old who gets a spanking on the diaper), turns into a non-effective approach as the child grows older. Spanking and hitting kids, more times than not, serves to release parental frustration instead of teaching the child any particular lesson. When this happens we are getting away from our primary parenting goal. What tools are we trying to give the child by hitting them? The goal of effective teaching is more difficult to reach. All we end up teaching our kids is how we respond when we get mad at them. Children confuse the lessons we are trying to teach them once hitting enters the picture. Lessons about compliance and respect get confused with lessons about how to handle anger and frustration. We really do not want to teach our child that hitting is an appropriate way of being angry, but this is often what they learn.

We look back on our parents and the spankings they gave us, and the loyalty we attach to this technique is amazing. I have heard hundreds of parents become nostalgic about being hit in their home when they were growing up. When I explored this phenomenon a little further, I found that even though the hitting was the discipline, the rules often continued to be broken. There is a truism we must attach to this: Adolescents will break rules and test limits, but I maintain that there are far more effective things that parents can do rather than use physical discipline. Please remember that hitting tends to lose its disciplinarian qualities past a certain age. Remember that hitting is the response of an emotional teacher, and, as you will hear over and over, **emotional parenting is, more often than not, ineffective parenting.**

Let me close with a final thought regarding spanking. When anyone sees a big kid beating up a smaller kid, the response is universal. One must come to the rescue and send the big kid running to pick on someone his own size. The fight is unfair, and the underdog is the recipient of much consoling and pity. Isn't the same thing true when a parent hits a smaller child? Doesn't the parent afterwards feel the need to console, and apologize, or, at the very least, doesn't the parent feel bad for a while, and maybe overlook the next rule violation because of the exaggerated emotional response that they gave over this one? When we physically punish our kids, we have probably missed an opportunity to apply more effective discipline.

This book contains examples and situations that describe more effective disciplinary techniques. Removing age-appropriate privileges and adding important incentives, and holding the child ultimately accountable for their choices is what **Unemotional Parenting** is all about. It encourages parents to understand where their child is, developmentally, and to make rational and effective parenting choices that coincide with this knowledge. This book will also help parents understand the importance of consistency and stability in their responses with their children. Most parents will find unemotional parenting a much more effective and rewarding technique than spanking.

CHAPTER TWO

Obstacles That Get In Our Way

IN CHAPTER TWO YOU WILL FIND

- The effective parenting philosophy
- The pitfalls of trying to control your kid's behavior
- The problem with being more invested in your child's choices than he or she is
- Personal responsibility: a tough lesson for teens to learn
- What to do when your child says he or she do not care about your imposed consequences
- What you should do if your kid gets worse after you start Unemotional Parenting
- The troubles that occur when parents do not work as a team

Now that we have identified the principal goals of parenting (i.e., to be a tool giver and an effective teacher for our children), we should discuss some of the obstacles that hinder us from being consistent and effective. Unemotional Parenting is a way of setting up choices for our children. We need to recognize that we cannot really control our kids behavior, but we should also realize that we can make it more difficult for our children and teens to make the wrong choices.

A common pitfall that stops us from being effective parents is when we become more invested in our child's choices than he or she is. For example, if you want your sixteen year old to respect her curfew, you should contract with her making clear the behavior that you want: "I want you to come home by 10:00 p.m". This verbal contract should outline the consequence that will follow if the teenager does not keep her end. "If you arrive home after 10:00 p.m., then you will be choosing to lose your weekend. You will lose your Friday night and your Saturday night out with your friends." The contract should also include a positive goal for the adolescent, such as: "If we can go this semester without you losing your weekend nights, then you will earn the privilege of increasing your curfew one half-hour. You will be allowed to stay out until 10:30 p.m. instead of the 10:00 p.m. time."

Now observe the difficulty of a parent who is more invested in the child's choice than is the child. The sixteen year old straggles in one night at 10:15 p.m.. The parent says to her, "I wonder why you chose to lose your weekend nights this weekend." The child gets angry: she makes excuses for being late, blaming everyone and everything except herself for her tardiness. She sulks around the house through that weekend, letting the parent know that she is angry. More importantly, however, the contract is fulfilled. **Good job, parents!** A few weeks later the girl again stays out after the curfew time. Again the parent says, "I wonder why you chose to lose your weekend nights this weekend." The child responds differently this time, however. She says, "Not this weekend, Mom - I have the prom. I am not going to miss the prom." Mom, who is now reminded that this is the prom weekend begins to think about the importance of the event, and the $150.00 that she has already spent for a dress and shoes, begins to renegotiate the contract. "Okay. You can go out on Friday to the prom, but the next two weekends you will stay home." This is the **wrong answer** and it is a good example of the parent being more invested in the consequence than the kid. If the teen were as invested, she would not have tested the parent and the curfew law. In this example all sorts of rationalizations may occur for the parent. Mom may think, *I can't expect my kid to be perfect; everyone makes mistakes.* Mom may overemphasize the importance of prom night, thinking, *Junior-Senior prom is a once in a life time deal, restricting my child from this* *would be unreasonable.* She may even think to herself, *She has really done pretty well with this rule. In fact I think that we may not even need the curfew rule anymore.* All sorts of things come up because parents want to be "reasonable." However, they allow emotional content into the contract, and thus into their parenting. If, as parents, we did not begin this renegotiation of the contract with the adolescent, how quickly do you think she would learn this curfew rule? It is likely that the teenager who missed the prom would sit around the house and try to make the entire house miserable that weekend because she was miserable. But don't you think she would have learned a valuable lesson about personal responsibility and about how her parents will remain consistent when push comes to shove? Isn't personal responsibility one of the tools we want to give to our children as they approach adulthood? An emotional parent would have missed this marvelous opportunity. An unemotional parent would have taken the step towards imparting this important tool to their child. Parents, you can substitute the prom incident described above with any number of things that will come up in your teenager's life. Other common examples of these types of incidents include: the concert tickets that have already been purchased, the homecoming football game, the Halloween party, the trip to Disneyland with the church youth group, and so on. When the parent becomes more invested in the child's choices than the child, there will be problems.

Let us look at the above scenario one more time. The sixteen year old has failed to hold up her end of a contract. She has chosen to violate or break a rule. If the mother allows a softening of her response, she will miss the opportunity to show her daughter how the real world operates. In the real world, things do not get easier for us because we fail; rather, they get easier for us because we succeed. If I could choose to break the speed limit in my car, and I would get a judge who is more invested in my keeping my money and not increasing my insurance rates than I am, I would speed all of the time. I would ask the judge to renegotiate the law every time I got pulled over for driving too fast. But the real world simply does not work that way. Do not teach your children that they can get what they want by breaking their contracts and making bad choices. It is your job as a parent to teach them the exact opposite lesson.

Sometimes the over-involved parent is more interested in their child's happiness than the child. Take, for example, a sixteen year old boy named Ralph. His mother and father rarely used the same parenting approach. Dad had an alcohol problem, and though he was recovering and sober, he frequently felt bad about the problems he and his drinking had brought to the family. Because of this, he let Ralph's mother do the majority of the decision making. Ralph also had a fifteen year old sister. She was a perfect child; she got A's in school, and never caused her parents worry about her friends. She never broke their rules. She allowed the parents to think that they were on the right track. After all, they were raising her well. Ralph, however, decided one day to drop out of school. His parents, who valued his education more than he did, were afraid of his quitting.

They came to me for help at this point. I began exploring the important things in Ralph's life. He loved his car. He had paid for half of it himself, and he was paying monthly insurance premiums. He had also put an expensive stereo into his car. Another important thing in Ralph's life was his job at the hamburger place down the block. This was where he had met his friends. Ralph had another interest. Ralph wanted to be a heavy-metal guitarist, and once he had dropped out of school he was planning to start practicing the guitar and looking for band members.

This took place in Colorado where mandatory education ends at age sixteen. If a child chooses to drop out after age sixteen, there is little anyone can do. I instructed the parents to utilize the important things in Ralph's life to make his choice to drop out of school a difficult one. They agreed that they would say to Ralph, "We know that we can not control your choice to drop out of school, but we want you to graduate. Therefore, if you choose to drop out you will experience the following consequences: first, the sale of your car, and the loss of the money from the sale. We will do with that what we wish. Second, we will call the Hamburger Junction, and tell them that you have quit. We still have the right to do this. Finally, we will give away your guitar and your amplifier. There is a recreational center nearby that would love to have such nice musical instruments. We know that you can still choose to drop out of school, but we hope that you will not make this choice."

At our next meeting, Ralph came in with his parents. He wore a broad grin. I asked him how school was going, and he quickly replied, "I dropped out." I turned to his mother. "That must be hard for you," I empathized. "Have you found a buyer for his car yet?" She stammered her response, "No, I think it's important for Ralph to have his car. . . I don't want to take him everywhere and, besides, he has paid for a lot of it himself." I began to feel a headache coming on. "How about the hamburger job?" I queried. "Well, Ralph needs to work, and we did decide to charge him $100 rent since he is no longer in school." "What about the heavy-metal band equipment?" "I couldn't give that away," Mom said. "Ralph has so few friends, and he would be miserable if we took his dream away." In this case, Mom was too involved with Ralph's happiness. She could not follow through on the hard part of parenting. Do you think that Ralph knew this when he was presented with the consequences attached to his choice of dropping out? Dad had the right instincts, but he let Mom do the parenting. Mom wanted to be liked by Ralph, and she was simply more invested in his happiness than he was. Mom's emotionality and Dad's disengagement resulted in poor parenting. Mom did what many parents do. She set up a consequence, and when push came to shove, she failed to apply it. Instead of making Ralph quit his job at Hamburger Junction, Mom changed her limit to "You must pay $100 rent." If Mom had followed through, and Ralph still dropped out of school, why would this still have been good parenting? Because she would have made it difficult for Ralph to make the wrong choice. Mom would have been a consistent role model and "tool-giver." When parents provide consistency, they have done good parenting.

I want to talk a little bit more about inconsistency. Parents become inconsistent when they feel that what they are doing is not working. They often jump around with a variety of punishments and rewards trying to find something that works. They lack confidence in their ability to set appropriate limits, and to back these limits up with appropriate consequences. **The approach of unemotional parenting is a confident one.** If you follow the philosophy of parenting I am discussing, you will gain back some of the confidence that you may have lost using your trial and error approach. Do not apply the principles in this book in a haphazard way. Do not try them one week and abandon them the next in hopes of solving the different problems that occur. When we jump around and try different approaches, kids gain a great equalizer.

The most common tool teenagers use in their attempt to get their parents trying something else is the "I don't care" response. For example, you ask, "I wonder why you chose to lose your stereo for one week because you chose to cut your fourth period algebra course today?" Your child responds, "I don't care. Take my stereo." He acts as if the stereo loss is unimportant. This makes his parents angry. They then think, *We'll make you care.* They either add more punishments, or change them. For example, the parent might snap, "Then you will forfeit the television." The child has his stereo back because he has convinced his parents that he really does not care about it. The following illustrates this very point:

EMOTIONAL AND INEFFECTIVE

PARENTS: We are tired of you skipping classes and getting calls from the school telling us about it. If we continue to get these calls we are going to ground you from your stereo.
TEEN: You can't take my music! That is so lame. Grandma gave me that stereo.

UNEMOTIONAL AND EFFECTIVE

PARENTS: We have gotten another call from the school attendance computer informing us that you have missed your fourth period algebra class again. You need to know what we will do should you continue to skip classes at school. If we get another call from the school, you will not have access to your stereo or CDs for one week. If we get a second call while you are on restriction from your music, you will lose your CDs for good. If your music has meaning for you, then do not choose to be restricted from it.

TEEN: You can't take my CDs. I paid for them. You guys didn't even give me that stereo. This is crazy.

PARENTS: We won't take your music unless you choose to have it restricted. It is up to you. None of this will happen if you get to class and quit skipping.

The teenager misses his class again, and the parents must now follow through with the consequences.

PARENTS: We got a call from the attendance computer. You missed your algebra class again. You are grounded from your stereo.

TEEN: Fine - take my stereo! I didn't even miss the class. I was late. It's not like you care. Take the CDs too!

PARENTS: If you don't care about your music, then try this one: you are restricted from the phone. Further-more, if you don't change your attitude, you are going to end up in summer school.

TEEN: What? Summer school! School sucks. I'm flunking algebra anyway; why should I go to that class?

PARENTS: If I had that attitude, how long do you think I would keep my job? I can't just decide not to go because I don't like it.

TEEN: Another lecture! (He angrily leaves and slams the door.)

PARENTS TO EACH OTHER: How long do you think we should restrict the phone? How about until he goes to school for one week without missing? Okay! We will tell him when he calms down a little.

PARENTS: We got a call from the attendance computer telling us that you ditched fourth period algebra again. We are taking your stereo and CDs for a week. Remember, if we get another call this week, you will lose your CDs permanently.

TEEN: You guys are ridiculous. Why don't you just take everything I have? I am flunking that math class anyway; why should I go?

PARENTS: If you need help with algebra, we can talk about getting that for you. Still, you knew the deal. It is still up to you whether you lose your CDs permanently. You have lost them for a week.

TEEN: I don't care.

In the above examples, you can see how more efficient and effective unemotional parenting is. Parenting is over when the unemotional parents give the child the message that they do not care either, but their consequence still applies. The emotional parents start to try to make the child care, and they end up changing their consequence. A few weeks later, when a different problem presents itself to them, they remember that taking the stereo and CDs did not work (and actually they did not even use these important items), and they feel frustrated. As parents we cannot get into an emotional struggle with our kids about whether or not they care about the consequence we apply. We cannot get into a struggle with ourselves about trying to make them care. As parents, one of our jobs is to know what is important in our children's lives. This is a full-time job because the things that matter to our kids change as they go through different stages. We know that the stereo is important to a fifteen year old because we see him listening to it all the time. When he is doing homework or when he is trying to fall asleep, his music is on. We know that his music is important because he spends a lion's share of money buying the latest CDs, and a fair amount of time talking to peers about MTV or the latest hits. Do not let the "I don't care - take my stereo" response stop you from picking this appropriate and effective consequence to your teen's bad behavior.

Another strategy that teens often apply to encourage their parents inconsistency is to up the ante with them. They behave negatively more frequently, escalating matters to test their parents' resolve. Parents naturally begin to feel that their approach is not working, using the evidence of their kids' newly found negative behavior as their guide. If the parents change their approach because of the teen's upping of the ante, however, they have taught him or her how to get back in control of the house. **You should be warned that your teens will do this "ante upping" at first, even if you begin to apply unemotional parenting techniques.** They have already gained a comfort zone with you and with your existing parenting style. They will try to get you back to your old parenting ways to regain this comfort zone. Don't give in! Believe that unemotional parenting will work, and demonstrate to your kids that you will continue to apply these effective strategies, regardless of what they do. Your children will come around after a final challenge or two, and after they realize that you are behind this parenting approach for the long haul.

The most obvious problem is that most parents think their children are different, and they believe that what may work for other people's kids will not work for theirs. Parents convince themselves that their child will not respond, or that he or she does not need such a drastic parenting approach. They need to remember that there is really nothing drastic about this approach to child rearing; it calls for parents to serve as role models who respond to situations not impulsively, but out of foresight and fairness. This new approach may take some time. Your children will need to be convinced that your old parenting approach will not return. To repeat an earlier point, your children may have grown comfortable with your parenting, and they may not easily give up this comfort. They will understand this change, however, when their attempts to get you back to your emotional ways fail, and they end up costing themselves things that are important in their lives. Many teens think that the power struggles that they engage in with their parents are a very important part of who they are. Many times these children will play a trump card to win a struggle. Many teens will threaten to kill themselves; they might take pills or make superficial cuts on themselves. Some kids run away, or at least threaten to. Imagine how difficult it is to be the parent of an angry adolescent who runs from home and tries to live on the streets. These trump cards, if played, can make any parent question themselves and their approach.

Parental consistency is doomed when the parents do not agree on how their goals are to be reached. **Parenting is best done when both parents work together.** This assertion sounds simple, yet it is only good common sense. Today, how common is it to have two parents in a home? What happens when you are a single parent,

and do not have the luxury of having a partner? What happens
when there are two parents at home, but one is a step-parent taking a subordinate role in parenting? What happens when the parents are in a bad marriage, and staying together for the sake of their
kids? Frequently these couples are unable to act as a team, because
their marital relationship is in such discord that agreement is
impossible.

Single parents often have a more difficult task, because usually they are trying to make up with the child for things like placing
them in the single-parent situation in the first place. Single parents
often try to play too many roles, and sometimes it is the role
switching that makes their parenting approach confusing. They
play the role of parent, confidant, best friend, bread winner,
provider, and male or female role model. Parenting is simply
tougher for the single parent, but it is not an impossible job. On
the contrary, the consistency that the unemotional approach offers
to all parents is probably even more important to the single parent.

Step-parenting comes with its own set of difficulties. The most
common of these occurs when the natural parent pushes the step-
parent into a subordinate role because the natural parent emotionally believes that their new partner does not really love the child in
the same way, and, thus cannot raise the child adequately. When
this emotional dynamic occurs, the child is able to split the parenting team, and the result is that the child often runs the show.
Another common problem arises when the step-parent criticizes
the natural parent. Often the criticism relates to the previously
failed marriage, and implies that the natural parent is incapable of
providing adequate parenting. Since he or she failed in the marriage, and since the child is presenting with problems, the implica-
tion of the criticism is that the child is in need of something "different". When parents struggle with each other about their roles as
parents, they make poorer decisions, and inconsistency results.

Divorced parents can also consistently parent their child. One
way for divorced parents to do this is to talk with each other about
trying to be consistent in both home environments. Remember -

just because your marriage has failed, your efforts as parents need not. Often this is the only bond that keeps the ex-spouses in contact with each other. If the divorce and the feelings surrounding it prevents the parents from developing a team approach, the custodial parent can use this approach to help with consistency and effectiveness.

How about the homes that have two parents? I encourage those parents strongly to look at their work as a team effort. It is only by consistent and efficient parenting that your kid will benefit. All too frequently, one parent will take a soft approach, and the other will be the harsher disciplinarian. This creates a vicious cycle, in which parent number one thinks parent number two is too hard, and acts to sabotage parent number two by taking the side of the child, or by softening the punishment. An example of this would be dad grounding the kid from his weekend plans, and mom allowing the child to go out on Saturday despite the grounding. When these types of things happen, dad ends up responding not just to the kid, but also to his wife. Dad most likely will also become harder in his approach to balance the softness displayed by mom. The child will then end up making most of his or her requests from the softer parent. You can see how you have quite a vicious cycle occurring here. All involved in this cycle end up losing, because tremendously ineffective parenting is the result. Yet how do you stop it from occurring?

Unemotional parenting challenges the parenting team to identify the goals of parenting and to establish a plan on how to reach those goals. I suggest that parents begin to approach their child as a team, not as individuals. Let me give you an exaggerated example of the type of parenting teamwork you want to set up. Your teenager approaches dad and asks, "Can I have that last piece of pie in the refrigerator?" Your typical response may be, "Sure, I don't care." The teen goes to the refrigerator and gets his slice of pie. Sounds simple? NO. Your response should be, "Oh, I don't know - let me talk to your mom and we will get back to you." Now the kid knows that you will make a parenting decision, not a unilateral decision. You go upstairs and talk to mom. She informs you that junior had two candy bars on the way home from school, and that he also had a milkshake at lunch. She also informs you that she was saving the last piece of pie for her snack tomorrow. In this situation mom offered information that was not readily available to dad when the child made his request. If dad did not gather this information, and junior got the piece of pie, mom would have correctly been angry. Now that dad obtained this information he can return to the child and say, "**We** have decided that you cannot have that last piece of pie." For many of the parents reading this, I urge you to consider your language carefully as you talk to you children. If you say things like "It is okay with me if it is okay with your father," you have set up the father to be the bad guy when the answer turns out to be "no". When you do this, you set up a split in the parenting team, and you give your kid the opportunity to take advantage of this split. Parents should talk as "we", not as "I" or "he" or "she." If you take even the most basic requests from your child, like the request for the last piece of pie, and approach these requests in this way, you will avoid being manipulated by your child. A more common scenario of manipulation is described below.

The teen says, "Dad, Mom said it was okay for me to have the car this weekend, if it is okay with you." Dad says, "Okay." Then the teen goes to mom and says, "Mom, dad said it was okay for me to have the car this weekend, if it is okay with you." It is not hard to take advantage of parents who do not talk to each other. If parents are reaching decisions together, and the kids know that they do communicate with each other, then children cannot split their parents to get their way. In fact, if the teenager described above had approached Dad first, Dad should have said, "Mom said it was all right with her? I'll have to go talk to her and we will make the decision together." Dad would then find out that Mom actually did not give her okay to anything. Mom and Dad have successfully stopped the teen in his attempt to take advantage of them. In this example, both parents would return to the teenager and say,

"Junior, I don't know why you told me that it was okay with mom for you to have the car this weekend when you hadn't even discussed the subject with her, but you now do **not** have access to the car this weekend. We really would have had no problem with giving you the car this weekend if you had been honest with us. You need to know that we make decisions that involve you together."

Parents do not have to consult each other on every decision from the slice of pie request to the request to take the car. To expect that level of communication would be unrealistic. However, if you begin your parenting consulting with each other, and your kids learn that you discuss parenting decisions together, then your parenting will become much easier. If one spouse is out of town or unavailable, you will be able to respond in a way that is consistent with this teamwork approach: that is, you will come to think like a team, and you will begin responding like a team.

CHAPTER THREE

The Advantages: What Parents Need to Know

IN CHAPTER THREE YOU WILL FIND

- Do you know what things are important in your child's life?
- Do you know your child's behavioral repertoire?
- Learning to set consequences before your child acts out
- Learning to talk to your child about their choices
- The control you have over the important things in your child's life

In unemotional parenting, there are three important things that parents need to know about their kids. The first important thing addresses the changes that occur during your child's emotional and cognitive development. Parents must always know what things are important to their children. Your child gives you this information daily, in how he or she spends free time. You must watch them, and observe them. Is your kid on the phone with their friends a lot? Is he or she in front of the television? Does your child hold down a part-time job that gives them spending money as well as a place to go? Is your child a video game addict? How important is your kid's stereo and music to them? What kind of music does your child listen to? Who are their favorite artists? How often do they watch MTV? Desserts and sweets are often important for younger children. Money has taken on increased importance in recent years, and it tends to become more important as the child gets older. Make-up and clothes become more and more of a priority as your daughter travels through adolescence. Spending time with friends or fixing up the clunker car they acquired are valuable observations about important things in your child's life. How about their curfew, and their freedom to spend time out of the house with friends? Are these things important for your child? What about sports and the latest school team they play on - isn't that an important item in your child's life? These sample questions are all reminders to you as parents to keep up your kids. When you come to the point of setting contracts with them, or removing privileges and adding incentives, the knowledge of your child's interests and activities can be used to your advantage. It does not make sense to use a reinforcer or consequence with something that the child no longer cares about. One of the advantages you have as a parent is your knowledge about what is important in your child's life. Do not ever give up this advantage. Your relationship with your child should make this advantage a very natural and easy one to obtain. If you are sharing in the important things in your kid's life you have this advantage.

The next parental advantage you have with your child is the advantage of predictability. You have seen your children respond to a variety of situations. You can guess how they are going to respond to new things that present themselves. When your children get angry, for example, you know how they show it. You have learned things about their veracity and trustworthiness. You have a history of their behavior that you can recall and make use of. When you know your child's behavioral responses and the choices they habitually make, you have a tremendous advantage. I am not saying that our son or daughter can't show you new behaviors, both positive and negative - they can and they will. I have already mentioned that when you make changes and become a more consistent parent, they may up the ante in their behavior to cause you to make emotional and inconsistent decisions again. They may show you behaviors that you have never seen before. What I am saying is that parenting becomes much easier when you are able to predict your child's response, or a range of possible responses. Parents must know their child's behavioral repertoire, and they must use this knowledge to avoid emotional traps. For example, if you child has run away, do not be surprised if he or she runs away again. If your child has ditched classes at school, he or she may do this again. If you child stays out past the time you have set for them to come home, it will most likely happen more than once.

For example, a daughter might be instructed to be home by 10:30 p.m. In the past she has only complied with this curfew request about half of the time. Each time the daughter has violated the curfew, the parents have become emotional and upset. They may have acted surprised, saying, "How can she be so insensitive to us?" They have held onto the hope that their daughter will no longer come home late, but they are still under the illusion that finding the correct parenting response to this problem will be all that is needed to put it to rest. Since these parents do this time and time again, they are not utilizing the advantage of predictability and the knowledge of their daughters behavioral pattern in their parenting. Instead, they stand disappointed and angry waiting at the front door for their tardy daughter to arrive. When she does shuffle in, they yell at her, and they tell her that she is grounded from her friends for a month! These parents hope and believe that their daughter will learn their lessons and not repeat the negative behaviors. When they are repeated, the parents sometimes act out of frustration and move angrily into the next parenting role. They begin setting consequences. If this is done while the parents are upset, they end up parenting by the seat of their pants. The point I am trying to make is this: as parents, we have often experienced our kids acting out against us, and we have often responded in an emotional manner. We have tried to set consequences for our children's behavior immediately following the rule violation, and have become ineffective because our responses have been emotional and inconsistent. Often we have overreacted in our anger, saying things like, "You are grounded for a year." Then, when time has passed and we have cooled down, we have usually backed off on limits like those. Both the children and parents know those kinds of responses to problems are exaggerated and unrealistic, and that they result in consequences that will not be followed through.

The feelings of powerlessness and helplessness that parents experience are also attached to this idea. Parents review the constant problem, and they remember the varied responses they have attempted, and they feel that nothing works with their child, that they have done everything possible, and that nothing has made a difference. Unemotional parenting will challenge you to plan appropriate consequences while predicting your child's responses, and to execute your parenting in an unemotional way. If you are able to establish consequences for your children's behaviors *before* they make you react to them, you will have increased your odds of being successful and consistent tremendously. You will be able to pick consequences and rewards that fit the behavior, and you will not have allowed your emotionality to dominate your decision making.

In unemotional parenting, one goal is to set the consequence for rule violations **before** the rule is broken, not afterwards. This reduces frustration on the part of the parents and increases their effectiveness. Skillful parents exert parenting energy *before* their children act out and break their rules, not afterwards. You can see how important it is to know your children's behavioral repertoire, so that you may address possible responses in an efficient way. Most parents put little energy into their responses until a rule is broken, and at that point they usually try to teach their child a lesson about the rule violation. Oftentimes they are ineffective as teachers because their teaching becomes entangled with anger and frustration. Setting appropriate consequences before a rule is broken removes the emotional conflict and makes responses clearer and more effective. More importantly, it also makes the child responsible for their behavior, as they know what will follow if they choose to break your rules. For example, if your teenager has begun skipping classes at school, you can handle this poor choice by establishing consequences before he or she engages in the behavior again. You may tell your teenager that the consequence for missing classes will be the removal of their car until they are able to attend for one month without missing. Now if your teenager skips class, your established consequence takes over, and your parenting is done. You can see how more efficient and effective this approach is to trying to lecture your child while frustrated, and establish a meaningful consequence while angry and disappointed in their skipping behavior. The teenager who knows the consequence for a behavior, and still continues to engage in that behavior, has only themselves to blame. The teenager who does not have an established consequence for inappropriate behavior frequently blames the parents for how difficult their life has become when they are punished. Personal responsibility is a difficult lesson to learn, but unemotional parenting is the best way to teach that important lesson.

Unemotional parenting also challenges you to stick to your guns and not to experiment with different consequences in an attempt to find something that works. When your child learns that you will respond in a predictable way, he or she will learn not to act in ways that result in having important things removed or restricted. This approach speaks to the way in which we communicate with our kids. Adolescents are at a stage developmentally where they want to be the authors of their own thoughts and actions. They resist having others tell them what to do or how to think. When we talk to our teenagers about the choices they have made, we are talking to them in a manner that is consistent with their developmental stage. When we talk to them about their choices and about the behaviors they have displayed, we are teaching them to take responsibility for themselves. Instead of lecturing children as to where they have gone wrong, we may substitute our emotional responses with questions. For example, when a kid comes in after his or her curfew, we may say, "I wonder why you chose to lose your Friday night out this week?" This is quite a bit different from arguing with the teen about why his or her curfew was set at 10:30 p.m. From the adolescent perspective, the latter approach can seem controlling, whereas the former implies that the kid is in control of his or her own behavior. We are simply wondering out loud why someone in control makes decisions that ultimately have negative effects on them. Another nice thing about this kind of discussion is that it ends our task as parents. We are done after we have informed the children of the consequences **they** have chosen. I will address this idea in more detail later.

What I am talking about here is, to a large extent, the most frustrating experience in parenting. You are trying to teach you child valuable lessons, and trying to maintain some kind of order in your home. Your kid seems bent on opposition and resistance to the order you want. He or she fights every limit you establish, and you end up getting frustrated because your expectations and the rules of your home are being violated over and over again. You wonder whether they are even teachable anymore when they enter adolescence and begin their rebellious phase. They are still teachable, but. . . **you must know how to teach them. You must know, given their developmental stage, how to get your lesson across.** When they respond to you and your teaching as if they do not care, and they repeat behaviors that you do not like, it is easy to fall into the trap of reacting emotionally. But if you know that your child will not always behave exactly as you would like them to, you will be better able to handle difficult situations in reasonable and consistent ways.

Parents have one final advantage - one which empowers them. Parents are still the major source of reinforcement for their children. I have outlined some of the current laws that make parents feel helpless (i.e., that teens can drop out of school at age sixteen, with or without parental consent, and that teens can seek out health services including birth control, abortions, and alcohol and drug rehabilitation without parental permission). Now it is time to discuss the law that empowers parents and will help them regain control over their homes and their children. Parents gain the advantage when they recognize that they are in control of the things that are important for their children. Parents own the possessions that their children claim as theirs: their clothes, automobile, money, make-up, telephone, stereo system, etc. Unemotional parenting helps the parents utilize this advantage. The leather jacket that daughter gets for Christmas from Grandma and Grandpa is really the property of the parent. The automobile that the sixteen year old is driving, despite how he or she got the car, is really the property of the parent. Even the job that the teenager is working is under the control of the parent. Unless the teen has departed legally from your home, or has reached majority age eighteen, the possessions that are so important to them are your property.

The law does require that parents provide for the welfare of their children. This means that we must provide shelter, food, and adequate provisions for our children so that they may thrive and grow. Automobiles, VCRs, cable t.v., money, expensive clothes and the latest compact disc fall outside the necessary provisions that the welfare law requires.

Responsible parents do not strip their teen down to one set of clothes and a cot to sleep on, and they recognize that children learn many lessons when they are allowed to have ownership. A teenager who is allowed to work a part-time job may learn about overtime, taxes, and the value of money. When the child loses a valuable possession they may learn to take care of their things in a more responsible way. The child who takes pride in his or her appearance and wardrobe gains a strong sense of self. These kind of lessons are invaluable, and an irresponsible parent who takes ownership of all the child's possessions to win power struggles is not taking advantage of their opportunities to get these ideas across. With responsible administration of rewards and consequences, the parent will feel more in control of their rules and their homes. Unemotional parenting teaches this kind of responsible administration.

In the next four chapters, you will discover how to implement the unemotional parenting philosophy into your home, The next section focuses on the developmental stages that your child experiences from the latency age through adolescence. Practical examples of how to use the parental advantages outlined in this chapter will follow.

CHAPTER FOUR

The Latency Stage

IN CHAPTER FOUR YOU WILL FIND

- Defining the issues of your eight to eleven year old
- What things are important for the latency age youngster
- Setting up a financial reward and punishment system
- What to do when children renegotiate your consequences and limits because things are not going their way
- Punishments that fit their crime
- An effective strategy to deal with kids that begin failing at school
- The struggle at this age around getting to bed on time

Pre-teens can offer a tremendous challenge to parents. In the latency stage (or pre-adolescent stage) which occurs between the ages of eight and eleven, your child is still emotionally, physically, and cognitively a child. Although they have experienced some of the pressures that will become crucial later on in their lives, they still rely on immature thought processes to sort through decisions. Parents remain an extremely strong presence in the lives of their children during this time period. The latency-age child will certainly test the parent and the rules they establish. Unlike the adolescent, however, these children do not purposely go against parents as a way of separating from parental influence. When the child is young, i.e., between the ages of two and eight, the major influence in their life is the parent. Parental approval and disapproval are major reinforcements and punishments. This is the period where kids believe their dad can beat up the heavyweight champion, and their mom can heal every wound with a kiss. Parents are the heroes of their young children for very good reasons: Parents hold all the reinforcements, they take care of all the child's physical needs, and they are large and powerful, with seemingly unlimited skills.

Kids from the ages of eight to eleven have a slightly different perspective. These more mature children have seen these seemingly heroic parents make mistakes. They are socially aware enough to know that other adults are out there, and that their parents do not have all the strengths and attributes that the child afforded them when he or she was younger. Dad is no longer capable of beating up everyone in the world, and mom makes mistakes. The hero role, in other words, becomes significantly diluted. Instead of having their parents as heroes, often the eight to eleven year old child picks other adults for their heroes and super-heroes. The four to six year old child often looks at fictional characters such as Batman and Superman for their heroes. By the time the child reaches latency age the Michael Jordans, John Elways, and Tiger Woods become substitute role models and heroes.

Parents have not lost total influence over their kid, however. In fact, they are still the most influential people for the latency-age youngster. Quite naturally, though, the parent now begins sharing their role and sphere of influence with others. Often teachers, coaches, and neighborhood adults gain influence with the latency age youngster. As we know, when the child leaves latency and enters adolescence his or her peers take on this influential role. Peers are important in the life of an eight to eleven year old too, but they do not influence the child as deeply as they soon will. For example, during the latency stage, if a newscast identifies an issue of controversy (i.e., a presidential election) the child will turn to the parent watching the show to get some bearing on how to think about the issue or the candidate. If the parent has strong opinions on the presidential candidate, the latency-age youngster, more times than not, will parrot these opinions. The same newscast with the middle adolescent will often produce the opposite result. The middle adolescent will disagree with the parent. The adolescent is concerned with separating from the parent, and the latency age youngster is still holding onto the family, and to his or her familial identity.

What things are typically important for this latency age child? I ask that you identify what is going on with your own kid, and use this next section to help you understand some other things that may be of interest for your eight to eleven year old. First of all, children at this age have discovered a new love for money. Previously the parents supplied everything for them, and their knowledge of value and belongings was limited. Kids at this age like to earn their own money, and they like to have some say on how it is spent. They also enjoy sweets, television time, video games, friends spending the night, and pizza parties. Kids enjoy family activities, outings, and physical activities. Sports and games typically are very important, even if the child isn't very good, or is not very coordinated. Children at this age are typically resistant to new responsibilities like added chores around the house. They don't like the idea that they are now old enough to do the dishes, or even the laundry, especially if these new tasks are introduced at this age. If the child has been doing some version of these jobs before the latency-age period, the parent usually does not experience as much resistance. Kids at this age rely on parents to take them places like soccer practices, after-school activities, and friends' homes. The parent becomes responsible for any trip that is inconvenient by bicycle, and typically the parent forgets that the taxi service they are providing is a privilege and not a right.

Behavioral contracts that often work with kids this age include a system that utilizes monetary fines and payments as punishments and reinforcements. You may want your child to keep his or her room in order. Payments of 50 cents per day for a made bed and clothes put away after school may be money well spent. Similarly, fining the child 25 to 75 cents a day for having a sloppy room may also make sense. I can't resist telling one more story about a nine year old and how emotional parenting failed, where unemotional parenting would have worked.

Mother wanted her nine year old to make his bed before school. This is an easy behavior to measure, so it is easy to establish a contract for it. The nine year old was a sweets hound, and he really responded well when desserts were at stake. Mom told her son, "If you make your bed, you can have the dessert after dinner; if you choose not to, you miss out on the dessert." This is a concise and easy contract to follow, don't you think? Mom came home one day after having a great day at work. She had gotten a raise for the project she completed for her company, she had received two compliments on her new hair style from her co-workers, and, to top it off, she had won $25.00 on a scratch lottery ticket when she stopped at the store on her way home from work. She came into Junior's room, and, of course, the bed was unmade. Instead of following through with the contract, however, she said "Nothing is going to ruin my day today. Come on, everyone, we are going out to dinner tonight. My treat". Dessert was served at the restaurant of course, and the whole family enjoyed hot fudge sundaes. Remember, Junior had not made his bed that day. On a different day, however Mom had a rough day at work. Besides getting a ticket from the local police on her way home from work for not using her turn signal, she ripped her dress on her desk drawer, and she had to lay off a subordinate employee that day for disciplinary reasons. When she came home after this long day, she saw that Junior had again not made his bed. This time, she called him angrily into the room and yelled at him, calling him lazy. She continued by telling him that he would not only lose his dessert after dinner that night, but also that he would not be able to go on the boy scout camp-out the following weekend.

As you know, both responses described herein were poor parenting decisions. Mom did not go through with the contract, and the kid did not know what to expect when he decided to let his bed go unmade the next time. The unemotional parenting response would have made more sense and made the parenting job much easier. Whether the mom had a good day, a bad day, or an average day, the young man would have encountered the same response: "I wonder why you chose to miss your desert tonight." When the child responds, he will most likely try to re-negotiate: "I'll make my bed now, I promise. Please, Mom, I love brownies and ice cream." Mom's response to the negotiating should be something like, "I am confident that you will make your bed tomorrow, because we are having a great dessert tomorrow as well. You have missed tonight's treat, and you know why."

Often, as in the above scenario, it is the parent that cannot handle the contract. The parent gets into changing the strategy and upping the ante, because they lack confidence in the fairness of the contract they have established. The kid may contribute to this lack of confidence by non-compliance, or by complaining and causing more emotional conflict within the parent.

Let's go back to some of the things that were described as important for children in this age group and put some unemotional parenting into action. Kids at this age are looking for fairness in their lives. They respond nicely to punishers and rewards that fit the behavior displayed. Prior to latency age children understand right and wrong solely on the basis of the end result of a behavior. The following example will clarify this point. Ask your five year old to tell you which kid was the most wrong in the following scenarios: *Johnny is five and he wants a cookie. His mother tells him that he must wait until after dinner for his cookie. The phone rings, and Mom leaves the room. Johnny decides to sneak a cookie while Mom is away. He climbs up to the cookie jar, and ends up knocking over and breaking the jar, spilling the cookies on the floor.* Scenario two: *Billy is five years old and he wants a cookie. His mother tells him that he must wait until after dinner for his cookie. Just then the phone rings. It is Grandma calling long-distance to talk to Mom. Billy's one year old little brother awakes from his nap and starts to fuss in the next room. Billy thinks that if he can get his brother a cookie, he will be quiet and mom can talk on the phone with Grandma. Billy climbs up to the cookie jar and ends up knocking the jar on the floor, along with three of mom's favorite dishes.*

Almost every five year old hearing these stories will tell you that Billy is more wrong than Johnny. They base their understanding on how many dishes were broken, and they do not take into account the intentions of either child. Latency-age children are able to look at intentionality, and they are able to understand the context where a behavior resides. Punishers that fit the wrong action are understood and expected with the latency- age youngster. When an irresponsible ten year old leaves his coat on the school playground and ends up losing it, what fair consequence should be applied? You really cannot make him live without a coat, but you may set up a way for him to replace it himself (i.e., having him do odd jobs in the neighborhood until it is paid for, such as shoveling snow filled sidewalks or helping his older brother deliver newspapers. Possibly giving him some extra jobs that you have around the house to work off the cost of the coat makes sense). Another fair punisher would be making the child wear last year's coat, which might be out of style or slightly too small, until he can earn enough money for a better replacement. Similarly, if the same kid rips or loses the socks that go with his baseball uniform, a consequence such as grounding really does not fit this crime; rather, you should consider as a punishment something such as making him play with other socks (even if they do not match his uniform, and even if they make him stand out from his other teammates), or making him replace his socks out of his allowance savings. Your goal is to teach him the value of being more responsible with his possessions.

The emotional parent below continues to respond to their child's irresponsible behavior by lecturing and inflicting guilt. She tries hard to teach the child a lesson about responsibility and taking care of possessions, but she does not really hold the child accountable for his mistakes in this area. The unemotional parent again has to do some difficult parenting, but in so doing is the better teacher. The effective parent has successfully applied the principle of picking a punishment that fits the crime, and the child is able to understand this punishment and learn from it. The child doesn't like it, but he does learn. See if you don't agree.

EMOTIONAL AND UNEFFECTIVE

NINE YEAR OLD: Mom, have you seen my socks that go with my baseball uniform? I have a game today.
MOM: No. Did you put them up after your practice yesterday like I told you to?
NINE YEAR OLD: Yes, I did. . . I think.
SEVEN YEAR OLD BROTHER: I saw Bowser chewing on something today that looked like your socks.
NINE YEAR OLD: What? Go get them.
SEVEN YEAR OLD: They aren't my socks.
The nine year old starts hitting and yelling at his younger brother.
MOM: Stop your fighting. I am tired of your constant fighting with each other. Do you want to go to the game or not?
NINE YEAR OLD: *(About to cry)* Not with these stupid socks. I will look like a nerd. I hate my brother.
MOM: You do not hate your brother. Get in the car and we will go to the sporting goods store and get you some new socks. I wish you took better care of your things. You just don't appreciate anything anybody does for you. You must think that money grows on trees or something.

UNEMOTIONAL AND EFFECTIVE

NINE YEAR OLD: Mom, where are my baseball socks?
MOM: Did you put them in your drawer after your practice yesterday?
NINE YEAR OLD: Yes. . . No. . . I don't remember.
SEVEN YEAR OLD BROTHER: No, you didn't. I saw Bowser chewing on them today.
NINE YEAR OLD: What? Didn't you take them from him?
SEVEN YEAR OLD: No, they aren't my socks.
The nine year old starts yelling at his younger brother. He begins pushing and hitting.
MOM: Stop your fighting. (*She separates them.*) Do you want to go to the game or not?
NINE YEAR OLD: I don't want to go without my socks. I will look like a nerd. Can you buy me some new ones?
MOM: No, you can earn some this weekend by taking on a chore for me.
NINE YEAR OLD: That is not fair. Billy saw Bowser eating the socks; he should have taken them away from him.(*He begins crying.*) I hate my brother.
MOM: Your socks are your responsibility, not your brother's. You know where to put your things. If they are important to you, don't leave them lying around.

NINE YEAR OLD: Mom, let's go. We are going to be late for the game.

NINE YEAR OLD: Everyone will laugh at me if I wear different socks. MOM: They won't laugh at you, but it is up to you. Do you want to go to the game with your regular socks, or miss the game and deal with the coach next week? NINE YEAR OLD: Let's go to the stupid game.

Another suggestion for a punishment that fits the crime is one for parents who have a latency-age child who does not turn in homework, or who otherwise has trouble with school: have an old jar on top of your refrigerator and label it "**DIRTY JOB JAR**". In this old jar put slips of paper with nasty and difficult household jobs written on them. For example, one slip of paper may say, "Pick up the dog poop in the back yard." Another slip may say, "Clean and sweep the garage." A third slip of paper may say, "Pull the dandelion weeds from the yard." You can use this dirty job jar as a negative consequence for a poor weekly school report. You can inform your child that he owes you two jobs from the dirty job jar when his weekly school report is bad. The lesson for the lazy student will be, "I wouldn't have to be doing this job if I just did my job at school." Remember, increased work responsibilities take away from the latency-age kid's free time and are often effective consequences. In this case they also fit the crime.

A simple assessment tool for parents is this: how does my kid spend his or her free time? You may then use this information as a source of both reinforcers and negative consequences to shape your child's behavior. Maybe you have a latency-age kid who is constantly fighting with you over getting to bed. To reduce the fighting, you may offer him or her this deal: "Whenever you can get to bed at the prescribed time without a struggle, you will earn a candy bar for you lunch the next day." You may also add a long- term incentive to this by saying, "I want you to save your candy bar wrappers because when you can turn in twenty five of them, you will have earned a trip to an NBA game, or to the pizza place with a friend, or to the video arcade at the mall". These are not such big prizes when you think about it. You get twenty five days of no fighting at bedtime, and the only cost to you are a pizza or a swimming pool trip! Another nice thing about this strategy is that now you can use the candy bar wrappers as negative consequences for other problem behaviors. For instance, you may say, "You will lose two wrappers if I have to tell you more than twice to do something like pick up your things, or feed the dog. What a consequence for the kid who has twenty one or twenty two candy bar wrappers and is looking forward to going to see his favorite basketball player with a good friend! If you take away two of these wrappers he will be a week away from earning that outing. All you have done as a parent is take two used candy wrappers, but your ten year old has learned to pay more attention to your requests. Candy bar wrappers have gained significance for him.

Unemotional parenting requires that you set up these types of contracts and parental responses to your child's behaviors before your child acts out. But what happens when the child's actions are not previously prepared for by the parent? Obviously, there are times that a parenting response is called for on a request from a child, or in response to an action by the child. **It is okay to delay your response. It is okay to tell your child that you and your spouse are going to discuss the matter at hand and come up with an appropriate answer.** Delaying your responses in these situations removes you from the heat of the battle, and allows you to continue to parent your child in an unemotional and effective way.

For example, what if your eleven year old was caught shoplifting from the local 7-11 store? You got called at work, and were informed of the situation, and you were asked to go to the 7-11 to resolve the matter. Unless this problem had presented itself before, this situation probably wasn't one that you have had set up a contract for. It was not a behavior that you knew exactly how to respond to. You became very angry and embarrassed because of your child's behavior. Now what does your kid require: a lecture on the evils of stealing, being grounded from activities, a fine, or a trip to the police station to get "scared straight"? It is okay to tell your child how angry and disappointed you are in his actions, and to tell him that you are going to think of an appropriate consequence to apply. You may also tell you son that you want to know what they think you should do. Gathering input from your child in these types of situations lets you know how they view their own behavior. Proceed with your consequences after you have had time to consider the action in a less emotional frame of mind. Talk with the other parent, or get advise from a grandparent, counselor, or friend who has had similar parenting challenges. You are trying to *teach* your child. Remember that an unemotional parent is more often than not the best teacher.

CHAPTER FIVE

Early Adolescence (Ages Eleven to Thirteen)

IN CHAPTER FIVE YOU WILL FIND

- Defining the important things in an early adolescent's life
- The dichotomy of age thirteen: one foot in the kids' world, the other jumping to become an adult
- Why do some intelligent seventh and eighth grade girls suddenly begin failing at school?
- An unemotional parenting structure that helps teens prioritize school work once again
- An effective approach in dealing with the youngster who is experimenting with alcohol, cigarettes, and other substances

What kinds of things are important for the typical young adolescent (children ages eleven to thirteen)? Girls this age are frequently getting into make-up and clothes. For boys clothes like sports team apparel and the latest cool tennis shoes become very important. The use of the telephone becomes an everyday occurrence, and sometimes an all-day affair. Music gains more reinforcing qualities, as MTV is frequently on the television, and the hottest group is played on the radio. Money gains even more importance because children at this age are too young for private sector jobs (i.e., fast food restaurants), but they like to frequent these places with their friends. Going to the local malls to hang out, staying out later at night, and being taken to activities outside the home are important events for kids in this age group. Friends become very important at this age, and though you really cannot restrict or control friendships, you do have some controls over where your kid hangs out. Transporting kids at this age to places is a major demand made on parents. Since evening and night activity is usually not appropriate for the eleven to thirteen year old, weekend days are used to meet many of their free time needs. Kids this age are burdened with increasing demands from school (i.e., longer and more tedious homework assignments), and demands from the home (i.e., regular work around the house). One can see why weekends become so precious.

We need to remember what is going on developmentally for children at this age. This is a difficult age because the teenager is leaving the child world and beginning their entry into adulthood. The fact is that they are not children anymore. Their bodies and newly activated hormones are telling them that they are growing up. Their peers are giving them the message that they are no longer little kids. But we know that they are also not adults. Their emotional and cognitive development are still a long way from being fully mature. The dilemma: the thirteen year old has really only known the child's world thus far, yet he or she is encountering pressure internally and externally to gain comfort in the adult world.

I met a thirteen year old girl in my practice that screamed at her mother one day because the mother would not let her go on formal dates until she was sixteen. The thirteen year old young adult insisted that she was old enough to go out on dates with boys, and that she had a sixteen year old who was showing interest in her. Mom had held her ground and informed her daughter that she was too young for this kind of social interaction. Later in the same session, this thirteen year old was arguing with her mother about the amount of work required of her around the home. Mom reported that all she required of her daughter was for her to pick up her own things in her room and in her bathroom. Mom then said, "If you don't keep your room straight, I am going to go in there and clean it up and throw things out." Mom mentioned that she was tried of stepping over her daughter's Doll. The thirteen year old little girl began to cry, because she thought her mother might throw away her doll. The same girl who was old enough to date sixteen year olds was sobbing because she thought she would lose a doll that was precious to her.

Parenting kids who are struggling with this issue is an extremely difficult task. If we try to keep them in the child world by not allowing age-appropriate activities in their life (i.e., allowing later curfew, more involvement with friends, and experimentation with make-up and hair-dos) they will resist with a resounding message: "I am not a little kid anymore." Their resistance may take on some serious forms. They may begin smoking cigarettes, drinking wine coolers, sneaking out of the home to hang around older teens, and becoming sexually active. If we as parents allow teenagers too much freedom and move them into the adult world too quickly (e.g., we don't provide them with adequate structure, we give them freedoms that they can not handle, or we lose touch with what kind of friends they have), they may respond with another resounding message: "I am not ready for all of this. I'm still a kid that needs structure." Though teens won't verbalize this second message, they may act in ways that request more structure in their world. They may begin smoking, drinking, sexually acting out, hanging around older peers, etc. in an effort to receive structure and discipline from their parents.

The struggle for parents of kids entering adolescence, then, is an obvious one: where is the balance between the need for freedom and the need for discipline and structure? To complicate the matter further, even the parent who does their job correctly may find themselves responding to a kid who engages in the behaviors described above. This is the beginning of the time when experimentation and high-risk behaviors show themselves. What is a parent to do? One suggestion to help you deal with this difficult dynamic is to get your child involved in appropriate and healthy activities such as sport teams, scouts, and church groups, in order to get through this stage with less high-risk behaviors from their teen.

Many parents who have daughters in the sixth, seventh, and eighth grades report that school grades begin to drop at this point. Many identify their kid as an A and B student in grades one through five, and now suddenly, their kid gets Ds, Fs and Incompletes. Oftentimes these parents do not report that school attendance is problematic, but they note that their daughter's performance in school has clearly dropped. It does not take a rocket scientist to understand what may be going on. The young ladies are putting more of their energies into socializing and impressing both female and male peers. Remember that clothes and make-up have now become important items in the eleven to thirteen year old girls' life. Young girls put a lot of energy into "fitting in" and into flirtatious behaviors associated with dating. School attendance does not accompany low grades as the new problem, because school is where the youngster is getting their socialization needs met. They are attending school, but they simply are putting their energies into socializing and not into academics. When they come home, instead of getting their homework done, they often head to the phone. This dynamic is not happening solely with the adolescent female, but it clearly becomes more pronounced in girls this age. They get behind in school work, but keep pace and even excel in the social arena.

Emotional parenting usually is very ineffective with the above scenario. Emotional lectures from parents follow each poor report card, and the child responds to the lectures by promising to do better the next semester. as well as making excuses about why their grades were so poor. Frequently, the adolescent blames the teachers or the classes. They may respond by saying, "That teacher is such a jerk. Practically everyone failed his class because he never explains anything." Or, "I didn't get to take a make-up test when I was sick last week, and that is why I failed." Excuses such as these place the blame for the failure elsewhere. The child is deflecting responsibility from themselves for not keeping up with the work. It is easy for the emotional parent to hook in with some of the excuses offered because, after all, their child has always done really well in school.

Emotional parenting often entails discussions about how good students find ways to get good grades even when the teacher is bad. Lectures to the teen about their future, and about how important education is to a good career, also accomplish little. Although there is no harm in expressing these thoughts, they alone almost never result in any behavior change for the eleven to thirteen year old. So why do almost all parents utilize these universal lectures if they yield such little results? One reason is that it make us feel like we are doing a good job, because we are expressing our values. We are teaching our kids verbally how really important school and education are. We feel good as parents until the next report card shows those nasty Ds and Fs, then we feel betrayed and ineffective.

Walk though this next example with me. Let's try some unemotional parenting, utilizing the important consequences in eleven to thirteen year olds' lives to make school performance take on more significance. Remember, unemotional parenting makes the kid responsible for their own grades and their own behavior. Also remember that as parents we really cannot make our child perform. We cannot control the choices they make, but we can make it hard for them to choose errant or poor behaviors. This is especially true with children at this age. Even though we have lost the physical control over them that we had when they were toddlers, we still have considerable parental leverage. Once again, the examples below delineate a more effective and focused approach (i.e., an unemotional approach contrast with an approach that is not very effective and oftentimes results in parental frustration).

EMOTIONAL AND UNEFFECTIVE	UNEMOTIONAL AND EFFECTIVE
PARENTS: What is happening to your grades? You have gone from As and Bs to near failing in one semester. THIRTEEN YEAR OLD: I hate my teachers. They pile on the work like I have nothing else to do except homework.	PARENTS: We are concerned about your school grades dropping. We feel that we need more structure at home to help you get your grades back to where you had them. THIRTEEN YEAR OLD: I'll do better next semester, I promise.

PARENTS: You spend half your time on the phone. We never see you doing any homework. What are you talking about?

TEEN: My friends are important to me; don't even think about taking my phone away.

PARENTS: Nobody said anything about taking your phone away; we just want you to spend more time on your school work. Especially in Math. This F doesn't cut it.

TEEN: I will. Math wasn't my fault. Mr. Jenkins flunks over half the kids every year. He is a terrible teacher. I hate him.

PARENTS: You are not applying yourself. Mr. Jenkins may be a tough teacher, but good students get good grades from tough teachers.

TEEN: I said I'll do better. I wish you guys would chill out and get off my back.

PARENTS: Don't take that attitude with us, young lady. And to show you that we are serious about you getting your grades back up, you are grounded for a week.

TEEN: Grounded for a week? Starting when?

PARENTS: Starting now.

TEEN: I was going to spend the night at Amber's tonight. We already planned it.

PARENTS: Too bad. You are grounded.

TEEN: (*Angrily*) I am going to go call Amber and tell her I can't come over.

PARENTS: We are counting on it, and that is why we want you home after school by 5:00 p.m. Dinner will be at 6:00 p.m. After dinner the television and phone will be turned off and it will be study time. At 8:00 p.m., when you are done studying, you can use the phone or watch television until 9:00p.m. Then you have forty five minutes to get ready for bed.

TEEN: No way! One hour for the telephone?

PARENTS: We don't like having to put this much structure in your life, but since you aren't mature enough to set limits on yourself, we are going with the above plan. When you get your grades back to Bs and As we will take this structure away. It is a matter of maturity.

TEEN: I said I would do better. Here we go again; you don't trust me. I said I'll do better.

PARENTS: It is not a matter of trust. When you can show us that you can maintain your grades, we will remove the structure. If you continue to do poorly, we will keep the structure in place. It is really up to you.

TEEN: What if a friend calls during study time? I can at least talk to them and let them know, can't I? What if I don't have that much studying to do?

PARENTS: If the phone rings, we will answer it and inform your friends that you will call them back or see them at school the next day. If you don't have two hours of studying, you can work on a project that is due at the end of the quarter, or review material that you are having trouble with. It will be school study time from 6:00 p.m. to 8:00 p.m.

TEEN: You are trying to control my
life again. I get it.
PARENTS: No, we're just hoping that
you will take control of your own life
yourself.

The ineffective emotional approach in the above example does
not really have a plan for addressing the serious problem of failing
grades. These parents are clearly winging it, and the teenager is
obviously in charge of the conversation. The teen declares in an
emotional way that the telephone will not be restricted. She also
places the blame for her grades on her teacher. The parents fall back
into old lectures, and when it is time to set a consequence for the
low grades, they fall back on the ever-popular "grounding."

The unemotional parents, however, have a plan that addresses
the problem. They keep control of the conversation in spite of several attempts by the teen to derail them. They have a structure set
up, and they use the complaints that the child raises as incentives
for her to make appropriate changes in her school life. These parents show concern by establishing limits. They have their child
checking in after school (and still allowing her to spend an hour or
two with friends after school), and they have a study time set up
without the distractions of the television or the phone. They also
allow an hour after studying for the child to entertain herself on the
phone or with the television. These parents are meeting both masters, so to speak. They are being respectful to their child's developmental needs, and yet they have a plan that is helping to direct the
child to more success in school.

Another skillful thing that the unemotional parents did in the
above example was to bring the notion of maturity and immaturity into the discussion. Remember, children at this age are trying to
show themselves and others that they have gained a degree of
maturity. Frequently you will hear from early-aged adolescents that
their peers are being treated better than they are. They will com-
pare themselves to their friends, or to their older brothers and sis-
ters, and remind you that these others have been allowed to do

things at the same age that they are not allowed to do these things. Challenging their maturity level by stating that you will reduce disciplinary structures when they prove that they do not need them is sometimes exactly the way to talk to your eleven to thirteen year old.

Kids at this age hate imposed structures, but they do seem to do very well when they are placed in a structured environment. When they resist your structure by not carrying out the prescribed activity (i.e., studying between 6:00 p.m. and 8:00 p.m.), then you impose consequences on them like restricting make-up, clothes, weekend days, or other things that are important to them. You know your child, and you know how they will respond to this new structure. You know that they will often resist the structure and resent certain aspects of it. You need to recognize this in advance, and pick an appropriate negative consequence for them if they choose to do this. Remember, there is already a positive consequence established if they respond favorably to the structure. They will earn more freedom, and the imposed structure will be reduced because they will have demonstrated the maturity necessary to balance their social needs with their academic requirements. One of the tactics of unemotional parenting is to identify the important things in your child's life, and then utilize these things as positive reinforcements when your child makes appropriate choices. The reverse, naturally, is also true. When your child chooses negative behaviors, then they should also be choosing to lose some of the things that are important to them. You cannot control their choices, but you can make it difficult for your child to choose certain courses of action.

The other essential element here is to set up these parenting responses before the child acts; that is, this type of parenting works best when you let your children know what consequences will be involved before they make their choices. Sometimes this is easier said than done. Sometimes your child will force you to parent them by showing you a behavior that is unexpected or new. I gave the example of shoplifting for the youngster in the previous age group. An example of this kind of behavior more common with kids eleven to thirteen is experimentation with cigarettes, alcohol, or marijuana. When the parent discovers a pack of cigarettes in their youngster's pocket or backpack they usually are surprised, and their natural impulse is to respond quickly. In the following example, you will again see how emotional parental responses are not as effective as the responses given by unemotional parents. It is not uncommon for the child to continually deflect blame off of themselves. The unemotional parenting team does not allow this to happen. They begin by discussing the consequence with each other before presenting it to the child. They develop a consequence that hits the child where he lives and that also fits the crime; in this case, lunch money and spending money. It tells the child that they will not support the habit of smoking, and again allows the child to make a choice concerning their own behavior.

Emotional and Uneffective

PARENTS: Junior, come in here. We need to talk with you. We found this pack of cigarettes and this lighter in your backpack.
JUNIOR: What are you doing going through my things?
PARENTS: You left your backpack in the middle of the floor, and when I went to pick it up, these fell out. You have some explaining to do.
JUNIOR: They aren't even mine. They're Doug's. He wanted me to hold them for him so he didn't get in trouble.
PARENTS: Well . . . we are going to keep these, and we're going to call Doug's parents to let them know that their son is smoking.
JUNIOR: Don't do that - everyone will call me a narc. Just forget about it.

First you go through my things, and
Unemotional and Effective

PARENTS: Junior, come in here. We found a pack of cigarettes and some matches in your coat pocket.
JUNIOR: What are you doing going through my things?
PARENTS: This conversation is not about us; it is about you having cigarettes. You know that we do not approve of this.
JUNIOR: They are not even mine. They are a friend's.
PARENTS: That may be true, but they are in your jacket, and there will be a consequence for this behavior.
JUNIOR: That is not fair. I told you they aren't even mine. What are you going to do?
PARENTS: We will discuss this, and we will let you know.

now you want me to be a narc on my friends.

PARENTS: You'd better tell Doug then. His behavior got you into trouble, and that's not what friends do for each other.

PARENTS: (*After discussion*) We have decided to take your lunch money for ten days. You can pack your own lunch. We don't know how you pay for cigarettes, but we won't support this habit. You won't get an allowance or spending money for ten days either.

A few days later the school calls the house and tells the parents that their child has been suspended for smoking on school property.

PARENTS: You have lied to us about smoking. The school just called and told us you were suspended.

JUNIOR: I didn't lie - those cigarettes you found were Doug's.

PARENTS: Well, you can kiss Doug good-bye, as you won't be seeing him again. You are grounded for the rest of the school year.

JUNIOR: Doug wasn't even smoking with me at school!

PARENTS: Who was?

JUNIOR:. Nobody. Why are you making such a big deal out of this?

PARENTS: You'd better believe this is a big deal. You just got suspended from school. Furthermore, we don't believe you or trust you. We will find out who else was involved. And you are grounded for the remainder of the school year.

JUNIOR: Why do you guys freak over such stupid things? Lots of people smoke, You both used to.

PARENTS: We smoked before we knew it was so dangerous. We aren't going to let you make the same mistake that we made.

JUNIOR: I wish you guys would get out of my life.

PARENTS: The school just called to tell us that you have been suspended for smoking. Since you started this behavior you have begun lying to us, you've become sneaky, and now you've gotten kicked out of school.

JUNIOR: I didn't tell you because I knew you guys freak out over this kind of thing.

PARENTS: We have talked over the consequences. While you are out of school on suspension, you will clean the yard, pull weeds, and paint the downstairs family room. You will work.

JUNIOR: Treat me like a slave.

PARENTS: Don't interrupt. We have some more to tell you before we will listen to you. We will not support your smoking habit. We cannot stop you from smoking, but we will not finance it. As we said on Monday, you will lose your allowance and you lunch money for as long as you continue to smoke. You will not smoke around us, in our house, or in our car. If you get into further trouble related to smoking, such as getting kicked out of school, or getting caught shoplifting cigarettes, there will be increasingly negative consequences. We hope that you will decide that it is not

worth it to continue to smoke and to
hang out with friends who get you in
trouble. It is up to you.
JUNIOR: See, I told you. I knew you
guys would freak.

The above example discusses the occurrence of cigarette smoking. It is an emotionally charged issue for many parents. With these
types of parenting issues it is easy to slip into an emotional mode
of responding. Even worse than the child being caught playing
around with cigarettes is the situation where the parents find out
or suspect that their kid has begun experimenting with marijuana
or alcohol. What would you do if a teacher called you and
informed you that your kid had come to school intoxicated? These
kinds of behaviors make us, as parents, react strongly. These reactions are usually clouded by frustration, anger, and disappointment. The tendency to overcorrect our children is strong, and, as I
mentioned earlier, this tendency may set us up of inconsistency. As
the examples described above, we may respond by grounding our
child for two or three months, or by telling them that they can no
longer see the friends that they've gotten into trouble with. When
our anger subsides, we realize that three months grounding may be
too much, and we negotiate an easier sentence with the child. We
realize that we cannot really control the friends that our kid has,
and if we do try to control them we get a teenager who begins lying
to us about who he or she is spending time with. We realize that
we cannot follow our kid everywhere he or she goes. We can't
watch them on the school playground during off hours, and we
can't follow them to the mall on the weekends. An emotional
response to the situation will most likely cause us to be inconsistent.

Again, remember that the best way to handle situations that
catch us by surprise is to tell the child that you are going to discuss
the problem and the consequences as parents and then get back to
them. A delayed parenting response is often more effective than an
immediate one. The one thing you do need to keep in mind when,

as parents, you discuss how to handle a difficult situation that has arisen is that **you must try to establish enforceable consequences.** Chapter eight will discuss strategies that help in establishing enforceable consequences.

CHAPTER SIX

Middle Adolescence (Ages Fourteen to Sixteen)

IN CHAPTER SIX YOU WILL FIND

- What developmental changes are going on with the fourteen to sixteen year old?
- The group of friends your child thinks are "cool"
- Self-esteem and the drug and alcohol group
- An unemotional parenting strategy that addresses the inappropriate romance of the eighteen to nineteen year old boy with the fourteen to fifteen year old girl.
- What to do when your teenager refuses to accept their consequence (i.e., a teenager who is grounded, defying the grounding and going out anyway)
- What ever happened to family leisure time in your home?
- The very high-risk behavior some teenagers display, tips on what to do when. . .

When children move into middle adolescence (i.e., ages fourteen to sixteen) they have a whole new set of issues to face. Usually by this age, your child has established a pretty steady peer group. It is not uncommon for the eleven to thirteen year old to try a range of peers to see where they fit in, but by fifteen or sixteen, however, they usually have a core group of friends who remain pretty consistent. Kids who continue to jump around (i.e., one week trying to fit in with the heavy metal group, the next listening to country music and wearing a cowboy hat and boots) usually have not been accepted by any specific group. Whether the cause is a lack of social skills, physical unattractiveness, or an inability to relate to group dynamics, these adolescents seem to have a particularly hard time in social settings. They often display low self-confidence and poor self-esteem. They often don't even have one or two close friends to help them through this difficult time in their lives. Frequently, these type of kids will find younger peers to be around. For example, consider a fifteen or sixteen year old who spends much of his or her time with his or her younger sibling's friends (i.e., children ages eleven to twelve).

A central issue for teenagers is the issue of fitting in. The teenager social network is complex and complicated. Teens often place a great deal of importance on popularity. Many adolescents are working hard to fit in with a perceived popular or "cool" group of peers. They choose music preferences, clothing styles, and extra-curricular activities on the basis of what is "cool" at the time. As the teenager begins fitting in with a group of peers, the group actually sets up a hierarchy. At the top of the group's hierarchy are the males and females who define what is "cool" for the others. These top dog teenagers are more popular, and have something that the rest of the teens either desire or wish to emulate. It is really sort of a dichotomy. Teenagers are seeking their own identity in the world, and in doing so, they are separating from parents and parental influence. It is dichotomous because they actively replace parental acceptance and family identity with peer acceptance and peer identity. Parents must recognize this awkward developmental stage as "normal", and avoid the power-struggles that will definitely occur if they try to define what friends and peers their kids can associate with. At ages fourteen to sixteen, parents are out of the loop when it comes to defining "cool" for their teenager. This falls clearly into the hands of other teenagers, and the social networks that are set up by same age peers.

Another way that these types of kids gain acceptance within a peer group is to attach to undemanding and often lower functioning peers. Many times adolescents without a core group of friends find the drug group at their school. The drug group does not require that its members possess very many skills. Usually, to get into the drug group, the only skill you need is the ability to smoke up, and to be antisocial to the teachers and adults in your world. This group pretty much will accept anybody who engages in these negative behaviors. For a teenager, unfortunately, being an active participant in a drug group stifles their social skills and their social development. They do not have to take many risks to see where they fit in socially. Without social risk-taking they often do not gain the appropriate social skills that they will need later in life. Other adolescent groups require some of this risk-taking. For example, if you are in the athlete group, you must be good at sports, or, if you are in the brainy group, you must be academically sound. The drug group requires no real social skills, and because it does not discriminate, it attracts kids who have low self-esteem and who do not feel that they fit in elsewhere. In the drug group acceptance is almost guaranteed.

Peer acceptance is the primary concern for kids between the ages of fourteen and sixteen. Unfortunately, this does not offer the parent any particular leverage or give them any strategies to follow. Oftentimes, parents try to control the adolescent's choices of peers and friends. This usually results in parental frustration and family discord, because most kids will not allow parental control over this important area of their life. Parents need to know how important peer acceptance and self-identity is for kids in this age group, because this knowledge will help them understand some of the pressures that their kids are facing. Parents will often find that oppositional behavior from their teen reaches new heights because of the social and interpersonal struggles that are going on with their adolescent.

Frequently, parents come to me with a problem regarding their kid's friends. They often leave my consultation unsatisfied because I tell them that involving themselves in power struggles over who their child can associate with is an exercise in futility. I inform them that it is unrealistic to try to choose their child's friends. There is one exception, however, that occurs with some frequency where I advise strong parental intervention. This exception is as follows: many times a middle-age adolescent female will hook up with older adolescent males. This feeds the young girl's ego and her desire to be more mature than her years. It is hard if not impossible, for the fourteen to fifteen year old girl to view the older male as her parents view him. The parents see him as a loser who does not have the social skills to attract a girl his own age. They view him as being interested only in sex and taking advantage of their daughter. They believe that he is using a younger female and the demands of her developmental stage to satisfy his self-serving desires. The adolescent girl, on the other hand, views him as the mature and "cool" peer who finally understands her thoughts and emotions. She may think of him as her confidant and her future. To support her position, she recalls that she has heard most of her life about how girls mature faster than boys. She can make perfect sense out of the match that has taken place from both a cognitive and emotional standpoint. If she becomes sexually active with the guy, her attachment to him grows even stronger. The act of sex for the young girl often serves to make her feel more seriously for her boyfriend. The young girls is ready to begin her sexual life from a physical standpoint, but emotionally and cognitively she is ill-prepared for this part of her life to begin. As she strives toward independence and adulthood, she receives the pressures that are placed on her to be sexually active in immature ways. In her attempts to grow up and to deal with the hormonal changes that are occurring within her, as well as the social expectations of her peers, she is "ripe" for a sexual relationship. When this occurs, she cognitively handles this important rite of passage by "falling" for her partner, thinking, "I have had sex with him, so I must love him." This tends to work in reverse in adult relationships in that most grown-ups tend to identify the attachment and the emotion before engaging in the sexual part of the relationship.

Naturally, parents become uncomfortable when their fourteen year old becomes infatuated with an eighteen or nineteen year old, and they should be. I have coached some parents to get the police involved in moving the eighteen or nineteen year old out of the relationship. In most states, statutory rape is defined as a sexual relationship in which at least four years of age separates the couple and one of them is a minor. Parents do not like getting police involved in these matters, and the police share this dislike. Many parents have been frustrated because the police have told them that unless the young girl files a complaint, or sex occurs without consent, they can do nothing. The above definition of statutory rape assumes that a mismatch has occurred. It assumes that a manipulation as a result of age has caused the sexual behavior. It assumes that minors cannot give informed consent to sex with majors. I have encouraged some parents to press this issue. I have told them to see the highest ranking officer in the local police department, and to review with him the situation that is occurring with their daughter. If the results do not change after speaking with a captain of the police force, parents may need to take the issue even higher. Parents can go to court to have a judge order that the police pursue this matter. Of course, this requires large attorney's fees, and an extended legal battle. In one case that I worked on, parents became frustrated by the inaction of the police and they did not have the resources to pursue their complaint in the courts. They went directly to the boyfriend and told him that they would file statutory rape charges in civil as well as criminal courts if he continued to see their daughter. Not knowing if the parents were bluffing or not, and having an eighteen year old's understanding of the law, this threat was all he needed to hear. He quickly left the fourteen year old alone, and more likely found another girl. This example is one of the very few scenarios in which I would support parents attempts to control peers and friends. Most parents who have tried to influence and control their teenager's selection of friends have found their efforts frustrating and unproductive.

How, then, do you discuss this emotionally-laden topic with your fourteen to fifteen year old daughter? It is a difficult issue, and one that rarely gets resolved without a lot of anger and resentment. The unemotional parent will be as straight forward as possible. The discussion will begin somewhat like this: "We need to talk to you about your boyfriend, and we know that it will be hard for you to hear what we have to say. It will be hard for you to understand our position, and we think that this discussion might get you so angry that you won't let us finish talking to you about it. We hope that you will be mature enough to hear us out, and we hope that you will not storm out of the room in anger because you disagree with us. We feel that you are not old enough to be dating eighteen and nineteen year old boys. We are not going to allow this relationship to go any further. We think, at your age, that dating someone that is four or five years older than you is very inappropriate, and your boyfriend is risking some serious legal charges by continuing to see you. If you care for him as much as you say, then you will not place him in the legal jeopardy that he can get into by continuing to go out with you. We are asking you to break this off now. If you choose to continue to see him openly, or if you try to start seeing him behind our backs, we will pursue these legal charges. As your parents, we ask that you choose not to make it necessary for us to do this. We love you, but we feel quite strongly that you are being taken advantage of in this relationship. We simply won't let this happen any more. We are going to have this conversation with your boyfriend. We are also going to hold you to your curfew, and if we find out that you have been seeing him after tonight, then we will get the authorities involved."

The parents in this approach begin by predicting that the conversation will be too hard for their daughter to hear. They predict that she will walk out of the room, or interrupt them and not let the conversation reach a resolution. When they do this, the odds increase that their daughter actually will stay in the room and not interrupt. This is a nice reverse psychological way of keeping control of the conversation. The parents then present their decisions in a straight forward way so that there is no room for misunderstanding. Their expectations are clear and easily understood (although almost never agreed with), and they incorporate the idea of the curfew structure.

Appropriate curfews, and a knowledge of your teen's outside activities (i.e., where they are going, whether they have adult supervision and having them check in when plans change) will prevent that fourteen year old female from relating to an older male peer. The structure and vigilance that you are providing for your fourteen year old will stifle the eighteen year old's advances, because there is usually little structure imposed in the home upon this older adolescent. Consequently, providing significant structure for your fourteen or fifteen year old will cut down on the ways that these different age groups hook up, and in this way it is preventative. If your fourteen year old must be in the house by 8:00 p.m. or 9:00 p.m. during the school year, and there are structures concerning homework time and other things, then they will not be outside hanging out with older peers. The eighteen year old will just be getting started with his night when your child is under your roof. Weekend curfews need to be more liberal, of course, to meet the developmental needs of middle adolescence. Having your adolescent come in at 10:00 p.m. or even 11:00 p.m. on weekends is not out of the question. Some communities have established curfew times, and you can utilize these times as rules for your child. Still, knowing your kid's plans and having the checking-in system in place are tools that will allow your adolescent their necessary freedoms while at the same time imposing your home structure on their activities.

Significant structure in the home is the preferred preventative measure against the bad behavior of your middle adolescent (i.e., ages fourteen to sixteen). Parents who do not provide significant structure for kids in this age group regarding school behavior, curfew, and after-school activities often experience the kind of problem described above. Sometimes it becomes a full-time job providing structure in you home for kids who are psychologically in a phase where they are challenging and fighting any and all limits within their world. Parents who have established adequate structures before their kids reach fourteen to sixteen years old will have an easier time of this phase than parents who are trying to establish a new structure in response to a behavior on the part of a fourteen to sixteen year old teen.

Remember earlier in the book when I talked about the differences between adolescent life in the 1990's and adolescent life a generation or two ago? Kids in this generation require more structure in the home that has been needed in the past. The world has become very dangerous for the fourteen and fifteen year old child. Today's schools often do not feel safe for adolescents. Drugs, weapons, and gangs are prevalent in many schools, and these dangers make teenagers long for security. In generations past, kids were not bringing guns and knives to school. They were not using dangerous street drugs between classes. They were not affiliating with known gangs, or fighting other kids because of the color of their clothes. Yesteryear, schools were more like extensions of the home. Schools practiced discipline for the problems that occurred there, and most children understood how the school would respond to any given problem they encountered. In short, the fact is that for many kids today, school does not feel all that safe. Naturally, then, home needs to be the place that feels safe. Feeling safe and being safe are directly related to consistency and structure in the home environment. When adolescents know what to expect from their parents, and they know that the structure the parents provide will meet their developmental needs, they will be able to move through the tough crises of middle adolescence. When the structure in the home is lacking, when the home feels no different that the schools and the streets outside, children will then tend to engage in more high-risk behaviors.

Many parents have experienced great frustration when they have attempted to implement the kind of structure described above. They feel helpless, anticipating the time when their kid decides to no longer comply with their requests. They might ask such questions as, "How do you handle kids when you ground them for a weekend night, but they go out anyway?" When your child's defiance to your authority grows more and more intense you might begin believing that there is nothing you can do. What is there for parents when their adolescents decide that they will do whatever they want? At these times, you need to understand what leverage you do have and what tools are at your disposal.

It may help parents to understand that when their children violate a consequence that has been established, these violations are simply new behaviors that require limits. That is If you tell your teenager that they cannot go out on Friday evening because they chose to violate curfew earlier in the week, and they go out on Friday anyway, this is simply another choice that the adolescent has made. As with the first choice of violating curfew, there needs to be an appropriate response from the parent to the teen's choice of going out while under restriction.

Parents own everything that the adolescent owns. The law is quite clear on this subject. Until your kid reaches eighteen, you are the true owners of his or her property. When children push the opposition button hard, you need to remember to use this leverage. I would never step into a boxing ring to fight the heavyweight champion of the world, would you? No, and the reason is that you can really be hurt. Parents sometimes fail to realize that they can really hurt their kids if the kid continues to fight over limits. Their choice is to fight your limits and your rules, and their choice to engage in power struggles with you may end up with them seeing where your leverage really lies. You can sell their car, take their stereo, give away their starter jacket, take their savings account, make them give up their part time job, and so on.

Most parents I have met do not push the fight this far. They don't like to restrict or remove certain things in their children's lives. Remember, in unemotional parenting you are not removing items of importance from your teen's world - they are choosing to have them removed by virtue of choosing to engage in the behavior that is the problem. It may also help you to remember that the alternative is even less desirable. If the alternative is an out of control young person who does whatever they want with a "screw you" attitude, you may want to consider a response that really "hurts" your youngster. When I describe this part of the parenting approach to parents, many report to me that they have tried to remove privileges and things of importance with their difficult teenager only to find that it did not work. Unemotional parenting is more than simply removing important items from your child. This is a fair and effective parenting philosophy that establishes parental consequences in advance of the child's actions. It will be successful only if you stick to this approach despite your kid's response to it. Lastly, this approach is more than a removal of privileges approach because it includes positive incentives for the child and the parent. I will say more about this in later chapters. Let me return to the situation where the teenager makes a choice to go out on Friday night while he or she is under restriction. When the adolescent, who is grounded on Friday night because he or she violated curfew, decides that you really cannot make him or her stay home that Friday, you need to consider removing something important in his or her life. Again, you will want to present this to the adolescent before they make the choice to violate your rule. You might say, "We know that we cannot actually keep you at home if you choose to go out. What you need to know is that if you choose to do this, we will remove your car for one month and if you continue to violate the consequences that you have chosen, then we will take it for good. We will sell it, or scrap it. You can decide if going out on Friday night after you have been grounded is worth that". Let me explain the logic behind viewing a child's antagonistic response to your consequence in this way.

Our society's legal system seems to operate in a similar way, doesn't it? If I choose to drive my car to Denver and I choose to go 75 miles an hour, then I will also be choosing the traffic ticket that follows. I will end up before a judge, and he will say, "This speeding ticket will cost you $50.00 and two points on your license." That is the consequence for my behavior. If I do not learn from this, or if I do not modify my behavior in light of this consequence, what will happen? Well, I will probably get caught speeding again, and I will go before a judge again. This time the judge will have my previous ticket to review along with the current charge. The judge will say something like, "Dr. Dixon, I see that you've gotten another speeding ticket. This one will cost you $100.00 and you will get three additional points on your license". He may also say, "Don't come back, Dr. Dixon, because another ticket is going to cause a suspension of your license". You see how the consequences are getting harder every time? Well, let me play out this example. Let's say that I get a third ticket, and I go back in front of the judge. Even if I beg, plead, and make excuses until I am blue in the face, the judge will be unemotional. He will say, "You do not seem to have learned from the consequences that this court has placed on you in the past. I am suspending your license for twelve months". Now I have been really hurt by my choices. I need my car and it has been effectively taken away from me. If I thought about these circumstances like an oppositional adolescent would, I might even convince myself that I will not get caught speeding for the next twelve months, and choose to drive without a license. I will drive and not speed, and I will be very careful to go the speed limit. Unfortunately, I end up getting caught with a tail light out, and I get pulled over. Now I have been caught driving with a suspended license, and the court knows how to handle this behavior. I get locked up for thirty days. The point here is that each time I violate the court's imposed consequence, they make it harder on me. They take each event as a behavior to be dealt with, and the court never feels powerless. They are never in the position where they have nothing they can do about my stubbornness and my lead foot driving.

As parents, we must act more like the court does in these cases. We must continue to establish harsher consequences, or make it more difficult for our teen to make poor decisions. Some teens may continue to make these poor choices because their antagonistic side is so important to them that they refuse to look at what it is costing them. Even more likely is that the kid may continue to violate the consequences established because he or she believes that the parent will not follow through on them. They believe that their parents will begin to feel helpless and lose confidence in their ability to do anything about the behavior in question.

Besides peer approval, other things that are important for kids this age include: later weekend curfew times, driver's permits and licenses, money, part-time jobs, clothes, music, dating, and activities outside the home. The phone is still an important item with kids age fifteen and sixteen, but in a strange sort of way, it has lost importance since the ages of thirteen to fifteen. The reason for this is obvious. The adolescent who is fifteen or sixteen is able to spend more time out of the home with their friends. They can drive and they have friends who have cars. The socialization that used to take place on the phone is being replaced by more face-to-face contact and activity. Parents of teenagers between fifteen and seventeen know that the phone is still utilized (in many cases too much so, but the importance for the phone has decreased). The adolescent now uses the phone less for talking than to make plans. He or she may still be on the phone a lot, but their conversations are usually shorter and more to the point. They want to get out and spend their time with their friends, and not simply talk on the phone with them.

Parents often handicap themselves when their adolescent reaches this age period. The teen is spending more time outside the home, and as a result the parents begin to spend less time with their son or daughter. When this happens, parents have a more difficult time identifying their kid's interests. If you lose the knowledge of your kids' interests and activities, then you will lose much of your leverage as a parent. It is helpful to know that, for most fourteen to sixteen year olds, CDs, stereos, concert tickets, MTV, and both structured and unstructured activities are important, but you should know specific things that matter to your son or daughter. It is helpful to know that many of the items that became important when your son or daughter entered adolescence (i.e., money, television, telephone, clothes, make-up, and so on) are still important in his or her life. These items and privileges will continue to be important throughout the adolescent life cycle.

Another common dynamic that occurs when kids reach middle adolescence is their experience that they no longer have any fun with their family. Oftentimes, adolescents describe their interaction with their parents as one that involves little or no pleasure. They often perceive the parents' demands as the source of the ultimate power struggle in their lives. Their free time is almost always spent with peers. When children are young, it is easy for the family to experience fun times together. Weekends are often spent in some family activity (i.e., going to Junior's soccer game, going to the swimming pool, having a barbecue in the back yard with neighbors, day trips to the mountains or beach, and so on). When kids are younger you often rent movies that are family oriented (i.e., Disney movies) and enjoy popcorn together in from of the TV. When kids get older they do not want to spend time with the family in this way any more. They often spend their time at a close friend's home or hanging out with their peers at the mall.

Parents tend to let this natural separation happen without much complaint. They begin to engage in the adult activities that may have been put on hold when their children were born. Adults now put their energy into getting their own leisure activity needs met. They may pick up golf or tennis, or use the weekend to run their errands or shop. The time that used to be spend in family activities is now spent with each individual doing their own thing. Frequently, mom or dad will feel this loss of family time and will make an attempt to return things to the way they used to be. I was working with one family in my private practice, and one day the following scenario occurred: Mom had suggested to her fifteen year old daughter that they rent a movie one night. The fifteen year old had agreed that it would be okay to stay home and watch a movie. When they went to the video store to make a selection however, they found that they could not agree on a film. The adolescent picked *Friday the 13th Part 5*, and her mother responded, "We are not going to watch that trashy film." Mom then reached for *A River Runs Through It*, and the teenager responded, "A movie about fly fishing in Montana? No way!" A power struggle ensued over how to spend the leisure time, and all involved got frustrated and gave up. The girl got her movie and watched it on the downstairs TV, and the parents watched the Montana fly fishing upstairs.

Family time is often a casualty to this developmental stage, but it does not have to be. The parent who finds ways to participate in their kids' lives by spending time with them in leisure activities is the parent that finds the disciplining part of their job more easily received. Remember, children often view their parents as the source of the ultimate power struggle in their lives. They perceive that the parent is only engaging in conversation with them when they have to set controls on them. "Why did you miss your algebra class?" "How come you got a D in your History class?" "Why haven't you picked up the garage like I asked you?" "Why do you hang around that loser?" These types of interactions feel like the extend of the relationship to the adolescent. Leisure time and family play time do a nice job in balancing this perception for the child. When this perception is modified, you will find that power struggles occur with less frequency and less intensity.

One area that I caution parents against restricting is the obtainment of a driver's permit and license. Clearly, our culture has established the age for this important event at sixteen. It has become an important rite of passage into adulthood. Ingenious parents often find that they can support this rite of passage by allowing their teenager to receive their permit and their license with no objections. Once a license has been obtained, parents are able to place restrictions on their teen's ability to drive. If the parent does not even allow their teenager to learn to drive, they set up a major power struggle in the home, as well as conflicts with peers, and even potential self-esteem problems. I encourage parents to allow their kid to gain his or her driver's license. Restricting the use of the car, or attaching rules to paying car insurance, are both reasonable limits for the parent to set. One of the most intelligent

approaches to the insurance policy issue is for the parents to negotiate a contract with their teenager. This contract often sounds
something like this: "It will cost us an additional $500.00 per year
to have you put on our insurance for our family cars. If you qualify for a good-student discount then it will only cost us $200.00 a
year. If you can maintain a 3.0 average, and qualify for the good-
student discount, then you will save yourself from having to make
an insurance payment of $500.00. If you do not, then you will
only be carried on our insurance if you pay the $500.00 premium".
This way, the teen is reinforced doubly for taking his or her schoolwork seriously. First, they get to drive. Second, they do not have to
pay higher insurance. Another important benefit is the increased
self-esteem that goes along with accomplishments in the academic
arena.

When your teens are able to drive vehicles, you are in a position to utilize this important function in their lives. The car is as
important as curfew, free time, and money to the sixteen year old.
It is much like the telephone for the fourteen year old, or the television for the eleven year old. Allowing your teens their drivers'
licenses actually affords parents more leverage and control. The car
then becomes an important teaching tool at the parent's disposal.

Emotional parenting for middle adolescent children often
occurs because parents feel frustrated and powerless. Many parents
have utilized the contract approach that I am writing about, but
they get stuck when they start to feel that it is not effective enough.
For example, oppositional fourteen and fifteen year olds will often
violate the consequences established on general principle. A parent
may restrict the telephone, only to find that the teen has ignored
the restriction and continued to call his or her friend. The scenario
described previously where a teen has been instructed to stay home
on a weekend night because they violated a curfew during the week
is very common. When the adolescent decides that they are going
to go out in spite of the consequence that has been applied, parents
begin to feel powerless. After all, what are they to do? In emotional parenting, the parents sometimes go overboard with anger, and
quite often try to overcorrect their teen. When the teen resists their

control, the power struggle continues, and the parents begin to
realize that they are not as effective as they want to be. I have
described how the court system in our society establishes harsher
consequences on the person who violates the original consequences. In the previous example, the courts applied appropriate
fining and points to the speeding driver, then had his driving privileges suspended, and finally he was locked up. Remember, that the
three prerequisites to this unemotional approach are: 1) knowing
your child's behavioral repertoire, 2) knowing the things that are
important in your child's life, and 3) knowing that you are holding
most of the reinforcers and punishers for your child. Parents should
discuss these situations before they occur. They should establish
enforceable and appropriate consequences for the teen that violates
their contracts and is hell-bent on doing what they want to do in
spite of the parental restrictions. If things come to the point where
the teen is supposed to be staying home, but they are deciding to
leave and to violate the established consequence, the parents may
have to use the heavy guns. Just like the court that takes away the
license of the violator, the parents need to utilize strong consequences for the child who displays this extremely antagonistic attitude.

Parents may take away valuable possessions, not just restrict
them. If the new CD player that the teen got for his or her birthday means something to them, he or she may need to know that
decisions to leave home while grounded may cost him or her that
CD player. Maybe the adolescent will respond with better behavior if he or she knows that the use of the family car will be jeopar-
dized for an extended period of time. Sometimes parents might
need to step outside the family resource pool to deal with a highly
oppositional teen. Utilizing police and runaway reports, or admitting your teen to day-treatment or inpatient programs may be
appropriate ways to handle severely oppositional behavior, especially if that behavior places the teen in dangerous situations.

I gave an example of unemotional parenting earlier in this
book about a middle teenage girl who violated her curfew and lost

her Friday night privileges. She then violated her curfew during prom week, and the emotional parent backed off on the contract. These types of parental responses are very common, and when they happen, they set the inconsistency ball in motion.

Again, unemotional parenting is easier when you can predict your teen's response to your behavior. It is easier when you understand his or her behavioral repertoire, and when very little can be done to fool or surprise you. But what do you do when your fourteen to sixteen year old pulls a stunt that catches everyone by surprise, displaying behavior that falls outside of your notion of his or her behavioral repertoire? For example, imagine what you would do if you discovered that your fourteen year old had taken your car for a joy ride around the block. When uncovering the situation you discover that he or she had crashed your car into a neighbor's tree. Fortunately, the fourteen year old had escaped unharmed, but naturally he or she had scared themselves to death. You begin to discuss this serious incident with your fourteen year old, and he or she tells you that they were only listening to the radio, and then they impulsively decided to take the car around the block for a ride. This kind of thing probably does not have a pre-established consequence. Not many parents would expect their kid to do such a bone headed thing. The following describes two ways of handling the same incident.

EMOTIONAL AND INEFFECTIVE

PARENTS: What were you thinking? I can't believe you took the car. Do you have any idea how dangerous that was?
FOURTEEN YEAR OLD: I know it was stupid, but I was just listening to the radio, and I decided to move it down the driveway. Then it kind of started going.
PARENTS: Listening to the radio! You could have killed Sammy! He was outside playing in his yard, you know.

UNEMOTIONAL AND EFFECTIVE

PARENTS: We can't believe you took the car. What were you thinking? You could have been killed!
FOURTEEN YEAR OLD: I know how stupid it was. You don't have to tell me.
PARENTS: We are extremely angry about this. We will discuss what happened and get back to you about what we are going to do. What do you think we should do?

(*Sammy is a 4 year old neighborhood kid*)

JUNIOR: I know. I told you that it was stupid. What more do you want? I feel bad enough already.

PARENTS: That is not going to cut it. You will come home after school everyday, and go to your room. You will come out only for dinner; no friends over, nothing. You will go back to your room after dinner. You can think about what you have done for the rest of this semester.

JUNIOR: I am supposed to go to the mountains with the science class in two weeks. Remember?

PARENTS: You can tell your science teacher that you are grounded. Maybe you can get your deposit back.

JUNIOR: Great. Now I am going to flunk science.

PARENTS: You are not going to flunk science. Lots of kids in the class weren't going. The mountain trip was optional. Most kids couldn't afford it and now you won't be able to.

JUNIOR: Yeah, but those kids had to do another project to make up for the trip. The trip is worth one third of our grade. I didn't do an extra project because I was going.

PARENTS: Well, you are not going. You had better find a project to do.

JUNIOR: I don't know. I guess I should be grounded.

PARENTS: Well, you can believe that there will be consequences.

Later, after the parents have talked, and discovered the physical damages.

PARENTS: Here is what we are going to do about the driving incident. First, there is a $250.00 deductible on the car damage before the insurance pays for repairs. You will work here and in the neighborhood mowing lawns until you have paid this off. Next, Mr. Simpson's tree is damaged. You will go to his house on Saturdays and help him replant, and put his yard back in order. You will also pay for whatever it costs to replace his tree. You will also apologize to the neighbors verbally and in writing. You said that you thought you should be grounded; well, you will be grounded until all of these things are done.

JUNIOR: I have some money in my savings. Can I use that?

PARENTS: Yes, but you only have about $150.00. You will have to work for the rest, and you will be grounded until all of it is paid off. The $150.00 will go to Mr. Simpson for a new tree.

JUNIOR: What about the science field trip at the end of the month?

PARENTS: Well, you had better get to work and earn the money for this damage if you want to go.

It is obvious that this kind of situation is laden with emotionality. If you try to establish consequences while in the heat of the turmoil, you will most likely make mistakes. It would be very easy to do while thinking about your fourteen year old on his driving rampage, potentially injuring or killing himself or others. You would also think about your car damage and envision your insurance rates going through the roof, and you would embarrassingly recall the damage to your neighbor's lawn. You would see the beautiful tree that he had that now needs to be replanted or replaced. You would realize that all of your neighbors and friends will begin gossiping and grading you on the lack of parenting skills that caused your fourteen year old to take this ridiculous risk. While all of this is going on in your head, what are the chances that you will decide appropriate consequences for this action immediately after hearing the news? In the above examples, the unemotional parent decides to wait before establishing consequences, whereas the emotional parent jumps right into the consequences. I believe that if you tell your fourteen year old that you are going to address the consequences with them after you have had time to think about the problem from all angles, you are on your way to more effective responses in your parenting. You do not need to bring a punishment immediately in these types of situations.

Your consequences may even start to take on a greater significance for your child if you do this. Imagine how anxious your teen might become while awaiting your final decision on the consequences for their actions. The fourteen year old may begin setting limits on himself in the interim. Consider his response if that night a friend called him and asked if he wanted to go to the NFL game the next weekend Certainly your child would not present you with this request, knowing how upset you are at his driving fiasco. Instead he will say something like, "No, I can't go this weekend. I'm sure that my parents want me to stay home." Delaying your parental response can produce some very effective discipline.

In summary, if you are unable to anticipate and put your parenting energy before your child acts out (i.e., by establishing a contract with your child around their behavior) because they have displayed a behavior that fell outside of their existing behavioral repertoire, or because the behavior in question could simply not have been predicted and parented until after it occurred, then delay your response. Delaying your response will assure more consistent and fair parenting.

CHAPTER SEVEN

Late Adolescence
(Ages Sixteen, Seventeen and Eighteen)

IN CHAPTER SEVEN YOU WILL FIND

- What are the developmental issues that the later adolescent is facing?
- The issue of leaving home rears its head
- Curfews for children who are almost adults
- The all-important automobile, a new parental teaching tool
- Moving from the role of a parent and teacher to the role of a coach
- Failure for our children: a difficult lesson for parents to allow
- Eviction and emancipation from the home
- Incorporating the input from your teenager into your parenting decisions

When teens move into late adolescence (i.e., ages sixteen to eighteen), they are struggling with an intense new issue. They become concerned with the approaching reality of leaving home. Parents also struggle with this issue. Even though we have generally defined the central conflict of adolescence as the drive for independence, the reality of leaving home is placed heavily upon teenagers as they move through their last year of high school. Parents lose their influence and their physical control as their children mature. When a teenager enters late adolescence, it is often the parents who struggle the most with the issue of their child leaving home. Jay Haley has written an excellent book entitled *Leaving Home* that describes the stresses that families and parents go through when a child enters this stage and begins addressing this issue. Parenting problems involving kids between the ages of sixteen and eighteen frequently revolve around issues of control. Parents have a difficult time giving up the control and influence that they have had with their child in the past. They have trouble redefining their parenting role, even though with teenagers in later adolescence, this is exactly what needs to happen. As teens approach adulthood, they need to gain a sense of the treatment that they will receive as adults. The structure you provide for the seventeen and eighteen year old should approximate the type of structure that he or she will experience when they are on their own. For example, curfews still make sense for kids this age, but they make sense for different reasons than they did when your teenager was fourteen or fifteen. For the younger teenager, a curfew is a needed limit that promotes their safety and helps to insure age appropriate activities. For the older adolescent, a curfew makes sense because these rules promote respect for others living under the same roof. The reason it is not okay for your seventeen year old to come waltzing into the house at 1:00 a.m. is because other people there are sleeping. The blasting of heavy metal music also requires limits because it annoys other family members living in the house. No landlord that I know of would allow other tenants to be disturbed by this kind of exhibition, nor should parents allow this in their homes. At the ages of seventeen and eighteen, a qualitative shift in the parent-child relationship is required. It is hard for many families to experience this shift because most of the rules that have been established in the home remain virtually the same. As stated above around the curfew issue, the rules may remain the same, but the reasons for the rules are different. A seventeen and eighteen year old is almost ready to be out on their own. The rules they are exposed to at home should parallel the rules of the "real world." When an adolescent is younger, they have curfews, limits concerning their stereos, and expectations regarding their school performance. Parents are required to shift in the way they treat their older teen. If the rules stay the same, the lessons that violations of the rules teach are different. A parent may expect solid work in school and appropriate grades academically for the young teenager because they are teaching the child about the value of an education, the rewards of hard work and self-confidence and self-esteem. The same parent may expect good grades and hard work in school from their seventeen of eighteen year old, but now it is because in just a short time, the real world will evaluate their work performance and their ability to complete what they have started in a very pragmatic way.

As we have done with the other age groups earlier, we need to discuss the things that are typically important for kids in the older adolescent age range. These things include the use of a car (either their own, or the family vehicle), money (which typically comes from a part-time job), music (as MTV continues to be influential on into later adolescence), clothes, and unstructured activities with peers. Telephone and television are still important, but as in middle adolescence, they are lower priority items than they were before.

Parents often find the sixteen to eighteen year old range quite difficult to negotiate. Sixteen year olds require more traditional parenting methods (i.e., contracting for behaviors or the removing of privileges) Eighteen year olds require much less. A parent who is frustrated with an immature eighteen year old may threaten to kick him or her out of the house for not following the prescribed limits. Parents frustrated with the acting out of a sixteen year old may want to kick him or her out of the home, but they will be unable to do this because of the child's age. The shift in the parenting role that I am discussing here will not happen overnight. Parents should have more control with their sixteen year old than they do with their seventeen year old, and more control with the seventeen year old than they do with the eighteen year old.

In addition to the leverage you gain in restricting the use of an automobile from your later-age adolescent, monetary fines can give you important leverages as well. Money becomes even more of an issue if the adolescent is earning his or her own spending cash at a part-time job. As with all of us, it hurts to get fined for bad behavior. When we get fined for traffic offenses, parking violations, late payments on our mortgage, or IRS penalties, these fines hurt, and because they hurt, they serve as effective punishments for the behaviors that cause the fines. How effective do you think a fining system would be with your teenager? If you fined a sixteen year old $15.00 for every class that he or she missed at school, for example, how much money do you think you would collect? If a $2.00 fine was established for inappropriate or vulgar language displayed in the home, how often do you think he or she would cuss you out? Of course, fining only works under two conditions. Number one, the teenager needs to have money and a source for getting more money, and number two, you need to be willing to take that money from the teenager (i.e., withdraw it from their savings account or paycheck). If your teenager can get pretty much any amount of money from you for the things that come up in their lives (i.e., a dance at school, a new movie, or a trip to Taco Bell with friends), then fining them is like fining yourself. Before you institute a fining system as a behavioral modification method, you must become very clear about what money means to you and to your teen. Money will have little significance if you provide everything your child wants. As stated earlier, losing money that has been earned is a much greater consequence than losing money for the sake of punishment alone. One last caution regarding fining as a punisher:

Set up your fining system before your child acts out. It is tempting to fine a teenager after the fact, but like with the other consequences described in this book, you must do this parenting before your kid has made their mistake. In the "real world" the fines that adults receive are all spelled out ahead of time. Every adult knows there will be a fine if and when they bounce a check, or miss a payment, or get caught speeding in their car, etc. Your teenager should also know what behaviors will cause them to get fined before a financial penalty is laid on them.

By the time your child is eighteen the parent should be more like a coach than a teacher. A coach is a useful source of information and support for the young adult. A coach is someone who offers experience, advice, and concern, but doesn't exert control. Certainly, every parent hopes that by the time their child reaches seventeen or eighteen, they will not need to restrict privileges as a way to gain compliance regarding house rules and expectations. However, since families and teens develop into maturity at different rates, this is not always the case. Unemotional parenting establishes appropriate consequences for behaviors that your young adult displays. You will maintain your parental advantage if you know about the things that are important in your seventeen to eighteen year old's life.

Our society tells us that our children are ready to leave home at the age of eighteen. They have moved from being a minor to being an adult. We know, however, that our job as parents is not totally over, and we know that just because our kids have eighteen chronological years under their belts does not mean that they are ready to function with total independence in the "real world". For example, most eighteen year olds are not prepared for responsibility like paying the first and last month's rent, or paying security deposits on rental property, paying for telephone and utility services, and the very real expense of food. Many eighteen year olds do not put limits on their own behavior, and they stay out late despite having to be up early for school or work. They burn the proverbial candle at both ends. Many eighteen year olds continue to display high-risk behaviors, such as drinking or doing recreational drugs. They may seek out casual sexual encounters and partners with little or no concern for the consequences of these encounters. These kinds of behaviors are common among eighteen to twenty year old people, yet our society tells us that our children are growing, and that we cannot take responsibility for all of their actions any more. If we as parents try to take responsibility and exercise control, we are faced with the knowledge that we really do not have the kind of leverage needed to do this.

Teens hate the notion that all of the possessions dear to them are actually the property of their parents. They feel that the law that gives their parents control over every thing they have is unfair. A sixteen year old can't fathom that the car he or she bought is legally the parent's car. Try to tell your fifteen year old that the Starter jacket that Grandma gave him for Christmas is really your jacket. They simply won't let themselves believe it.

Likewise, parents may hate the notion that when their kid turns eighteen, and gains major status, the law referred to no longer applies. Parents are unable to take their eighteen year old's car if it is titled to the eighteen year old, and they can no longer touch his or her savings account or stereo system. At eighteen years of age, the law says the possessions of the teenager become the teenager's. Parents can, however, tell the eighteen year old that they are on their own if they do not abide by household rules and expectations. Eviction becomes the major leverage parents acquire when the teen hits eighteen, taking the place of possession grabbing.

Jim Fay and Foster Cline have written an excellent book, *Parenting Your Teen with Love and Logic*. In it, they discuss how parents often deny their children the opportunity to experience natural consequences for their behaviors. An example of this would be the case of an eleven year old who decides that it is too much trouble to put on his coat before going to school. Instead of allowing the child to experience the natural consequence of being cold, and learning the functions of a winter coat, the parent rushes the coat to the school as the temperature drops. Another example is the situation of a kid who forgets his homework, and instead of allowing the child to get a zero on the assignment, the parent drops it by the youngster's homeroom so they will get credit for it. A very common occurrence is one where the child says he is not going to eat dinner, and at bedtime the parent allows him or her to make a sandwich. When kids are able to make their own choices, and allowed to fail with some of them, **they learn.** Cline and Fay emphasize that this learning can occur when a kid is very young. In fact, allowing kids to learn from their failures makes tremendous sense, especially at the age when the cost of those failures is relatively small. This dynamic is still operating even when your teen turns eighteen. By this time, however, some of the costs of their failures and bad choices are not as small. When your child turns eighteen, what more natural consequence can be applied for not abiding by house rules than eviction? As the reader can see, the cost of failure has increased from getting cold because of choosing to not wear a coat, to being forced out of the home for choosing not to abide by household expectations. Many eighteen year olds continue to defy the expectations of their parents because they know that their parents will not actually evict them. If this is true, then it becomes a question of whether the leaving home is affecting the parents more than the teenager. Are the parents forgetting the coaching role that they are supposed to be engaged in?

Eighteen year olds often use their new found adult status to their advantage with their parents. They often state: "I'm eighteen: I should be able to come and go as I please. I'm not a little kid anymore; I can do what I want." Parents, by contrast, are often afraid for their kid as he or she rushes to face the cruel, hard, and expensive world on their own, and they begin to feel powerless to help them. They have lost leverage and influence with their child. In some cases the most powerful leverage the parents have is letting teens know that they are indeed adults who can come and go as they please, but who must nevertheless abide by their house rules as long as the live with them. Many eighteen year olds leave when they hear this ultimatum. Often they will live with a friend, or live in an apartment with a roommate, and show their parents and the world that they can make it. Considerable problems can present themselves if the young adult crashes in his or her attempt to make it in the world. For example, if your eighteen year old's roommate moves out, or he or she loses a job, the teen's financial burden will become impossible. How should parents treat an eighteen year old who wants to come home again? It seems to me that there are two reasonable things parents can do. Number one, they can inform these children that they are on their own and that they need to turn their situation around by themselves. This is hard for most parents. On the other hand, they now have a great opportunity to re-establish a contract including household rules (e.g., how much the eighteen year old should contribute financially, and which household chores he or she must perform, the time the teen needs to be home at night so that other family members can sleep, or the time frame in which the eighteen year old must become gainfully employed). These will be the prices for returning home. The problem with number two is that this approach has already failed once causing the first eviction. When the eighteen year old returns, he or she often feels that circumstances beyond their control are the only reasons that they are not free of their parents. Frequently, an eighteen year old returning home responds to his or her parent's limits for a very brief time, but before long the parents are back in the unenviable position of initiating eviction procedures again.

At age seventeen, an adolescent is often behaving and responding like an eighteen year old, and parents do not have the leverage of eviction, legally, at this point. Often, parents with rebellious seventeen year olds start counting down to their kid's eighteenth birthday. The most obvious leverage tool for the parent to use with their sixteen and seventeen year old is the use of a car. Seventeen year olds have developed their school behavior pattern and they have a strong core of peers that they spend time with. Parents who try to change a seventeen year old's success at school, who try to have input concerning a seventeen year olds' peer group, are fighting an uphill battle. Sixteen and seventeen year old adolescents structure their days around their friends, their school, part-time jobs, and their families. The priorities for teens at this age reflect that order; that is, they spend more time with friends than with school, more time with school than in part-time jobs, and family time seems to come in low on the priority list. This is one way that the later-aged teen is separating and emancipating from his or her family. Seventeen year olds drive everywhere, and removal of this privilege remains the most important leverage point for many parents.

Even though you have lived with your child for sixteen or seventeen years, they still can surprise you with their behavioral choices or their requests. The strategy identified earlier in this book of delaying the parental response remains an effective strategy for dealing with this age group. For example, what if your sixteen or seventeen year old son asks you if he can go to California for a summer job to pick grapes in the wine country? The job pays well, but he will be gone for two months during the summer. What if your teenager asks you about transferring schools? What about the sixteen year old who wants to go to a heavy metal concert that does not end until 2:00 a.m.? You know that the band he or she wants to see has a reputation for promoting "partying" and "getting high." What can you do about these things? These types of requests require thought and input from others, and some conditions need to be agreed upon before any decision can be reached. Informing your teen that you will gather more information on the subject or you will discuss it with the other parent before making your decision are important steps in a thoughtful and legitimate course of action.

When teenagers reach sixteen or seventeen, your parenting decisions and choices remain important. The older teen is developmentally in a good spot. They can make your parenting much more simple if you have used unemotional parenting. They can participate with you to some extent in the limit setting process. They often can identify reasonable consequences for breaking rules, and they can pretty much abide by the rules that are set up if they are allowed to help in establishing them. I dedicate an entire chapter (Chapter 10) to this concept and strategy later in this book. Letting your teenager in on this requires that you treat them more like adults than children, and that you let go of some of the control and authority that you have established over the years. You need to listen to their input and try to incorporate their wishes if you hope that they will incorporate yours. It is at this time in your child's life when he or she is sixteen or seventeen years old that you begin to move from being an active parent, to being an advisor or coach.

CHAPTER EIGHT

Setting Effective Limits

IN CHAPTER EIGHT YOU WILL FIND

- Setting up enforceable limits and consequences
- Grounding: is it overused?
- How to make "grounding" really work
- What makes the consequences you establish unenforceable
- Varying your consequences as teens vary their behaviors: a different problem requires a different solution
- A word about "controlling" your child's behavior: remembering that they ultimately make their own choices

Earlier in this book I made reference to the idea that the consequences you establish must be enforceable. Parents often establish consequences that are unrealistic, or more accurately, unenforceable. Some examples of these include, grounding your teenager for extreme lengths of time (i.e., three to six months, or longer), taking away television or telephone privileges when you are not around to enforce this consequence, or the removal of driving privileges, followed by requests upon your teen to run errands for you. Let's examine why these stated limits often fail.

Emotional parents will sometimes ground their teenager for prolonged periods of time, but they usually do not identify the specifics of what it means to be grounded. Grounding takes many forms, and when it is used as a consequence, it should be defined specifically and clearly. Does it include going places after school? Does it mean that both weekend nights the kid must stay home, or that they cannot have friends over to the house? Does it mean that they are grounded from the phone? What exactly do you mean when you tell your teenager that they are grounded? When you use this consequence, and you establish a long period of time in which the grounding restriction applies, you make carrying out this consequence very difficult for yourself. Oftentimes a scenario like the one described below occurs.

A fourteen year old girl was grounded for two months because her angry parents had found out that she was smoking pot at school. They did not specify what being grounded meant, and the fourteen year old began discovering loopholes around this limit. It began to happen about one week into the grounding, when she asked her parents if she could go to a movie with her older sister and her older sister's friend. This was a gray area because mom had only wanted the girl to stay away from the kids who were engaging in the drug use. She also did not want her daughter to continue to pout around the house out of anger over being grounded. So she let her daughter go to the movies. Then, about two weeks later, the fourteen year old asked if she could go over to another friend's home, one that mom did not have concerns about. The mother let this occur too. After all, she wasn't really still angry with her daughter, so as a way of letting her daughter know how reasonable and understanding she could be, she let her daughter go. The rest of this story is not too difficult to figure out. The fourteen year old did not go to visit the friend that she had permission to see; instead, she went back to the peers who she was grounded from. She again began smoking pot. When she came home high, finally, she met with a furious mom and dad. They laid into her in the same emotional way that they had previously. Lectures about trust and the evils of drugs and restrictions from friends were again utilized to try to teach this difficult fourteen year old. The parents grounded her for another three months, and here is where it got even more confusing. Did this new grounding mean that the girl had the original grounding of two months (where five weeks still remained) to complete before the three month grounding started? Did it mean that she began her three month grounding now, and got an early release from the two month grounding? Neither the parents nor the kid answered these questions. Again, the frustrated parents did not specify what the grounding meant, and the fourteen year old waited about a week before defining the grounding on her own terms. In this family, the anger and emotions surrounding the misbehavior lasted about a week, and slowly the daughter began to make requests after these emotions subsided.

Another common occurrence in these kinds of situations is when teenagers feel that their punishment is too long and they develop a "sentenced to life with no chance of parole" mentality. They begin to do whatever they want to, because they believe that all their parents will do is add more time to their grounding (which they are not complying with in the first place). Then, of course, it becomes a natural reaction for the frustrated parent to say, "There is nothing I can do. I ground her, but she does not stay grounded. She does whatever she wants to do, and grounding her does not work." This cycle is completed with a frustrated and powerless parent who is ready to give up.

Shorter but more intense groundings are usually more enforceable and more effective. The teenager often learns the valuable lesson that the parent is trying to teach. It is imperative that you define exactly what the grounding entails. For example, you could say, "You will come home from school and go to your room. You will not have phone contacts or privileges. You will spend the weekends with the family at home. You will not have phone contacts on weekends, either. This grounding will begin today, and go through this weekend, next week, and the following weekend. You will regain all of your privileges after the following weekend." Questions like, "Can I go to the movies with my older sister?" or "Can I go to another friends home?" are answered in the negative. "Absolutely not. You are grounded until next Sunday." This seven to ten day grounding is intense because it involves most of the things that are important in a teenager's life. It involves the loss of free time, time with friends, after-school and phone privileges. Groundings that only take away one or two of these important privileges are less effective because the child can fall back on the activity left open to them for a short while without really missing the other activities.

What I am talking about is setting up consequences that are enforceable. If you ground your teenager from the phone, are you aware that there are times that he or she can get on the phone without your knowledge? How about when you restrict the television from your child? I knew a father from my private practice who knew that his twelve year old loved to watch TV. The twelve year old did not like to do homework, however, and many problems occurred around his choice to simply not study. Dad decided to ground his son from the television when he did not do his homework, but the twelve year old had the last laugh. He simply watched his shows while dad was gone and turned off the television when he heard dad pulling up into the driveway. He effectively diluted the negative portions of the consequence. Dad established a consequence that he did not or could not really enforce.

Some kids will respond to consequences in less manipulative ways then have been described above. Some children will simply not watch television, or will not use the phone when they are restricted from these activities. Unfortunately, not all kids are very compliant with these types of punishments. **As parents, we must be able to enforce the consequences that we have set.** Some parents are able to disconnect their phones when they are not home; others have actually taken the television with them to work. Still others respond to their children by letting them know that if they choose to talk on the phone or watch TV as long as these privileges have been revoked, they will lose even more significant things as a result. All of these strategies are effective and appropriate. The point is that our consequences must be enforceable. If they are not, then parents are reduced to simply hoping that their consequences will have an impact. Establishing enforceable consequences goes a long way in removing the "hoping" aspect of parenting, and insuring that the lessons you are trying to teach are actually learned.

Remember the example of Ralph. His parents especially his mother hoped that he would stay in school, and in attempting to guarantee this they established consequences that they had no intention of enforcing. They were able to set good consequences such as the removal and sale of his automobile, the termination of his job at Hamburger Junction, ant the giving away of his musical instrument, but they were emotionally ill-equipped to follow through with these consequences.

Some consequences are unenforceable because they are logistical nightmares (i.e., telling your sixteen year old that he or she is not allowed to drive when you need him or her to transport your nine year old to school everyday). Some consequences are unenforceable because emotionality enters into the equation, and as parents you feel that you are unable to do what you have said you'll do. Some consequences are unenforceable because you are not able to monitor whether they are being adhered to (i.e., the twelve year old who watches TV while dad is at work, and turns it off when he comes home). Another example of this kind of unenforceable consequence is the fourteen year old girl whose mom restricts her make-up because the daughter has been caught shoplifting lipstick and eye shadow from a department store. Mom tells her that she will be make-up free for three weeks, and adds that she will have to do ten hours of extra work around the house to "work off" her debt before she will get the use of make-up back. Mom is unable to enforce this appropriate consequence initially, because the daughter simply has a friend bring her make-up to school. She then applies her friend's make-up in the school bathroom before her first period, and washes it off before returning home at the end of the day. When mom finds all this out, it is by total accident. She goes to her daughter's school one day to pay for her yearbook and sees her "made up". Mom appropriately looks at this behavior as a "new" behavior, and, just like a judge treating a traffic offender, she offers new and more severe consequences for her daughter. The daughter now loses her new leather jacket. The daughter is informed that the make-up restriction will be extended another three weeks, and that if she chooses to violate this consequence again, she would lose her stereo. The daughter is also made to pay her friend's mother $20.00 for the make-up she has borrowed.

Mom in this case has done several things right. She has informed her daughter that if she chooses to evade established consequences and punishers, more severe ones will follow. She keeps the make-up restriction, and does not feel helpless or give up around this important item. She establishes punishers and consequences that are age appropriate, and applies them in an unemotional way. She makes use of the peer influence on her daughter by making the girl return money to her friend's mother. In this situation, the friend's mother applies some negative consequences on her own daughter for her involvement. Finally, the mother lets her daughter know that she will check on her, and that she will apply consequences that the daughter is well aware of if she continues to engage in this sneaky and manipulative behavior. Lastly, mom makes her daughter's choice painful. She loses a $150.00 leather jacket that means a lot to her, and she does not get it back. This daughter learns a significant lesson about her sneaky behavior and her manipulations. Mom successfully decreases the probability that her daughter will violate established consequences later. Mom also goes a long way in reinforcing values for her daughter. The girl learns that sneaky manipulation does not get her what she wants. Perhaps next time, her approach will be more honest and straightforward.

Another very common mistake that parents make concerns the notion of using the same consequence as the punishment for many different behaviors. Many parents ground their children because they come home late, but they also ground them for not doing their chores, for getting poor grades, for cussing at them during a fight, and for having cigarettes in their jackets. Do you get the point? It is very difficult for most parents to vary consequences for bad behavior, but it is essential that they do so. Things that make varying the consequence difficult for parents include: 1) not know-ing what other consequences may work, 2) finding a consequence that works with a particular adolescent and simply overusing it, and 3) emotional parenting, or not having a consequence that fits the crime. Cussing at the parent during a fight is not quite as important as bring home F's on a report card, finding out that your teen is smoking is not really the same as having them come home fifteen minutes after a set curfew. Behaviors that are not equal require different parental responses. Finally, a fourth reason why varying consequences is very difficult is that it makes parents work harder. It makes the mother and father talk together. They must talk about fairness, harshness, and the possible solutions to the cur-rent problem. They must become a parenting team and communi-cate about their children and their children's behavior.

It may be hard to reach the ideal of having one consequence for every behavior, but different behaviors do require different con-sequences. It you are going to ground your teenager from their Friday and Saturday evening activities because they violate the established curfew, then you shouldn't take away their Friday and Saturday evening activities for other reasons. Many potential con-flicts can arise if you do.

For example, Susie was told that if she came home after 10:00 p.m. during the week, she would lose her weekend nights. One day, Susie was caught smoking in a bathroom at school. Her par-ents were furious, and they took away her weekend nights for a month. What do you think the odds are that Susie continued to come home during the week before 10:00 p.m. (the original behav-ior that mom and dad were trying to correct)? Since she had already lost her weekend nights for a month, Susie became angry at her parents. She now figured that she could stay out until when-ever she wanted during the week, because, after all, what were her parents going to do about it? This made her parents revise their curfew violations contract (even though they had the lateness prob-lem licked prior to taking away Susie's weekends for smoking at school). Power struggles over Susie's time out of the home ensued.

Susie's parents, who began searching for another way to deal with her blatant curfew violations, became angry with her. Susie responded in kind, and began acting out in all sorts of ways. The parents only real mistake was knowing that Susie's weekend nights were precious to her, then, over- using this consequence on several different behaviors. If they had chosen a different consequence to deal with the smoking in the bathroom, they could have kept the weekend restriction for the curfew issue. An example of an effective but different consequence that the parents could have used for the smoking behavior might have been: "We do not appreciate your smoking, and we will not support a habit with our money. Now, instead of giving you lunch money to buy your McDonalds' hamburgers and Taco Bell tacos we will pack your lunch. We will not allow you to spend lunch money on cigarettes. You can have three months of bologna and cheese or peanut butter and jelly sandwiches in a brown bag to take to school." They may add: "You also will have your allowance withheld for three months. This means that whenever you want money you will have to ask us for it, and except for buying cigarettes you will be allowed to spend your money however you want. Your freedom to simply spend $10.00 at the mall will be restricted, unless you inform us exactly on how that $10.00 will be spent." In this example, Susie's parents are not telling her that she cannot smoke, but they are trying to make it very difficult on her to make this smoking choice. She may simply have a network of friends who give cigarettes to her, but her parents are saying that they will not support this habit, and at the same time letting her know what leverage they really have on the things that are important to her.

The parent who is able to pick appropriate and varied consequences, and to apply them to each different behavior, will be the most successful. **The axiom that every problem requires its own solution is the principle at work here.** Many parents believe that they simply are not creative enough to identify so many different consequences. Remembering the consequences are best identified and applied in the absence of an emotional reaction may help. I encourage parents to review the problem behaviors that their teen has presented to them at a time when there will be little or no emotional reaction. Here are some examples of common problems that require different solutions: 1) problems keeping curfew, 2) problems doing expected household chores, 3) foul language, and 4) poor performance in school. Now brainstorm with your spouse about what consequences should be applied to each behavior. The consequence must make sense, it must have an impact on the teen, and it must try to fit the crime. You may, for example, fine Junior $1.00 every time he uses profanity towards you. Or you may have him lose the next night out if he violates curfew. You may have him pick dirty jobs from your dirty job jar if he doesn't do his chores in an appropriate and timely way. You may restrict his free time, or his involvement in after-school activities (i.e., sport teams, part-time jobs) until he gets his grades up to speed. All of these consequences are different because the problems that they are correcting are of different importance.

If you are unable to brainstorm with your spouse and come up with more than one or two responses to your teen's behaviors, then your parenting will be much tougher, and thus less effective. If you continue to over utilize one or two punishments for the multitude of problem behaviors that present themselves, you will not remain effective for very long. Picking one consequence to apply to two or three different behaviors is better than having only one consequence for four or five different behaviors. The closer you can get to a 1:1 ratio, the better.

This chapter is about establishing enforceable consequences. Let's return to Ralph and his family once more. Mom and Dad have been unable to enforce the established consequences for Ralph's choice to drop out of school. They are emotional parents, and even though they have been coached in applying unemotional parenting techniques, they simply do not follow through. You have read two-thirds of this book; do you believe that the best parenting decisions are made when you reduce your own emotional investment and output? Do you believe that the best parenting occurs when you talk to your teenager about the choices they have made, and do not get drawn into the adolescent's game of blaming you for being the cause of the consequence that has been established? Do you believe that personal responsibility can only develop when you hold your child accountable for their choices and behaviors? The point here, again, is that your response as parents is vitally important. Many unenforced consequences are not really unenforceable, but they become unenforceable because the parents lack the courage to be consistent. Like Ralph's parents, and the parents who won't enforce the Friday evening restriction if it falls on Prom Friday, the problem seldom lies with the teenager.

CHAPTER NINE

School Violence
When the Unthinkable Happens

IN CHAPTER NINE YOU WILL FIND

- Multi-modal factors that contribute to tragedies in our schools
- How Parenting affects the social climate of violence. Prevention starts early. Get involved...
- The teens struggle for independence at home and desire for interdependence at school
- Some clear warning signs we as parents need to be aware of
- The two types of mistakes parents make who see warning signs in their child
- How to help your child make sense out of the senseless acts of terrorism and destruction.
- What Parents can do to stop the madness.

Over the past several years this nation has experienced a new, but very tragic and scary phenomenon in our schools. Communities in Washington, Illinois, Mississippi, Kentucky, Arkansas, Pennsylvania, Tennessee, Oregon, Virginia and most recently Colorado and Georgia have had to deal with the aftermath of teenage violence and terrorism. Emotionally unstable adolescents have engaged in killing and maiming fellow students at the schools they attend. They have planned and carried out acts of terrorism and murder on their own peer group. In a Littleton,

Colorado high school thirteen were killed, another thirty injured, and two thousand other students terrorized. The Colorado community and the nation were left to ask millions of questions in an attempt to make rational, the irrational acts of April 20th, 1999. On March 24th 1998 , it was Jonesboro, Arkansas where five were killed and ten others wounded by two student snipers who pulled a fire alarm at school, and waited for children to enter the crosshairs of their rifle sights. Back in 1988, in Winnetka, Illinois the first documented gun tragedy of this ilk occurred at a school . This one not perpetrated by a student, but by a mentally ill woman who bursts into a second grade classroom and opens fire. Eight years later in Moses Lake, Washington a fourteen-year old student began what has become all too common place in our society. Students killing students. Then on October 1, 1997 in Pearl, Mississippi the community is rocked by an unstable teen who began his murder spree at home before taking it to a local school. West Paducah, Kentucky followed just two short months after Mississippi's tragedy. Edinboro, Pennsylvania occurred only one month following the Arkansas shooting. Fayetteville, Tennessee had their killings on May 19, 1998, this tragedy was followed just two short days later in Springfield, Oregon. Then only three weeks passed and Richmond, Virginia dealt with the aftermath of a fourteen year old student taking out his anger at a classmate in a crowded high school hallway.

When these tragedies occur, people want answers. How could it happen? Why did it happen? Could it have been stopped? Who or What is to blame? People are seeking simple answers and solutions to a very complex problem. There are many aspects of our society that deserve scrutiny.

The entertainment industry along with television and the main stream media get scrutinized. Did you know that by the time an average teenager in our society reaches sixteen he has seen in excess of 16,000 murders on television? He has also seen countless rapes and lesser acts of violence. The music industry is filled with recording artists who sing about violence, suicide, sexual assault, crime and destruction. The video game industry literally makes millions of dollars annually by improving the graphics on games that involve fighting and killing. How much does this influence the lack of respect for human life, and lack of respect for social order?

Is the main stream media also responsible? Families in Edinboro, Pennsylvania, as well as Springfield, Oregon and Richmond, Virginia and Atlanta, Georgia may make compelling arguments that the killings that preceded theirs were overdone by main stream media coverage. Did copy cat killing occur because of overdone media exposure? The fact is, the media takes a story and presents that story ad nausea. The media will show human pain and suffering from as many angles as it can. They call it news. They justify it by saying "It is what the people want". There is a strong possibility that it is what the crazy gun men want. How much do they influence the lack of respect for human life, and the lack of respect for social order?

The access to guns and fire weapons also becomes heavily scrutinized. Teens today have access to guns. Laws to make guns illegal for teens are on the books, but ask a teenager if they know a friend who has a personal weapon, and the answer will most assuredly be, yes. The killers in Colorado made their own bombs. School killers in other cities simply had to go to their own homes to find their weapons. Others argue the opposite side. They argue that the criminals have guns, and the law abiding do not. They argue that making guns available to the law abiding will reduce the amount of senseless violence and killing from the criminal element. Whenever the type of tragedy occurs that occurred in the above ten cities, the role of gun access is heavily scrutinized. How much does the access of guns influence the lack of respect for human life, and the lack of respect for social order?

Drugs and Alcohol contribute. The drop out child often medicates with substances. The killers do not necessarily engage in the violence while under the influence of a substance, but there is increasing evidence that the psychological profile of many of these killers includes substance abuse or dependence. Illicit substances have also evolved, and teens today appear to have a nonchalant approach to the illegalities of using such substances. Underage drinking, marijuana use, and other substance use such as crystal methamphetamine (speed) are casually viewed as O.K. by many of today's adolescents. How much does this influence the lack or respect for human life, and the lack of respect for social order?

Teens today accept everything. Or so it seems. Gangs have infiltrated the schools, and very few teenagers that I am exposed to have much outrage about this. Instead, there seems to be a teen culture of generalized acceptance for the violence that is occurring around them. I am not saying that after a massacre and tragedy, the teens are not deeply affected. They are! I am saying that many adolescents know about other kids bringing weapons to schools, they know that some have guns in their lockers, that others are smoking marijuana during break periods, and they see the violent threat of other students in anger. Strangely, these teens seem to go through school passively allowing these behaviors to go on in front of them. Is the teenage culture of acceptance to blame? How much does this influence the lack of respect for human life, or the lack of respect for social order?

Teachers and schools are to blame! How can you teach a student and not know about their level of depression, and their level of emotional instability? Why don't schools have successful programs to help high risk kids? Why isn't there discipline in the schools anymore? Mostly the schools suspend or expel troubled kids, which causes further feelings of alienation, and most likely contributes to the anger that is directed back at the school and its participants. What about security? Why isn't there better security? Would metal detectors solve this problem? Should we hire police officers to patrol the hallways? These questions, and these accusations are levied at the school system *after the fact*. How much does this contribute to the overall lack of respect for human life, and the lack of respect for social order?

There are many other aspects of our society that receive commentary and evaluation. For instance, a society built on materialism and greed places objects and things above human life. Removal of God from the schools receives attention. . It has been said, that the only time religion and God are allowed in the school is when people are killed. It seems going to one's knees after a tragedy is all right, but allowing God into school when things are relatively calm is a no - no. Paul Harvey in a news commentary stated, and I paraphrase, "If we spent less time thinking about how we can keep guns out of our schools and more time thinking about how we can put God back into school, this problem would not exist" Then there is commentary about technology and other desensitizing events that we as a society allow. Things like; abortion on demand, or, cameras on our bombs so we can see how they hit their target on the evening news, and, Dr. Kevorkian practicing medicine by killing his patients, etc. Lastly, the juvenile justice system and department of social services receive criticism. Social Services because they are perceived as the governmental force that stops us from disciplining our children effectively. The juvenile justice system is viewed as ineffective because the impression is they take adolescent offenders and do nothing with them. Clearly, after tragedies occur in our schools, there is no shortage of social criticism and commentary. Only a shortage of plans to make change! All of the above topics receive heavy scrutiny after a school tragedy. No topic however, is criticized or scrutinized as heavily as the area of Parenting. The scrutiny first turns to the parents of the killers. I think we do this so that we can distance ourselves from the killer and his roots. We do not have to take responsibility for the tragic events if we can place the blame somewhere else. Ultimately, we the parents are responsible. We are the primary tool givers and teachers for our children. If we do not teach them that love, compassion and respect are important, then, they may not learn that they are. If we do not teach them how to resolve differences and conflicts, they may take it upon themselves to resolve problems with unnecessary violence. We are the role models for our children. If we are unable to accept this responsibility, then how can we expect our kids to learn how to take responsibility for their choices? We must now realize that our children are dependent on us. And we have to accept that our well being, happiness and welfare are often dependent on how others raise their children. If you doubt this, ask a family member of a slain victim.

Maybe Parents are the most heavily criticized because we play a part in almost every other influence that has been described above. We let the movies, the music, the video games etc. come into our homes without much effort to stop or change it. We criticize the schools our kids attend. Then we do not get actively involved to insure that the schools are teaching our children the lessons and values we support in our homes. We are into the materials acquisition race. We think that if we get our kids more than we had as kids, this is good parenting. So, we are happy to supply the latest computers, the finest stereos, the nice automobiles, and the college funds, mistaking these actions for good parenting. We argue that God should be part of the schools, and we neglect to have God as a part of our everyday existence. And the mistake that we make that contributes more than any other is the one we make when we neglect to take part in our child's life. This should not start at adolescence, this should start at conception. Showing our children how very important they are to us is a parent's job. At Columbine high school in Colorado, two students who felt they did not belong killed 13 others. They dressed for years in black trench coats, wearing make-up and nail polish. They spewed anger and hate towards the other cliques in the school, and they gathered about twenty friends who did the same. They planned for over one year the mass destruction that they eventually carried out in April of 1999. They even participated in chat rooms on the internet, and created a WEB site of their own which advertised their plans. Where were the parents? Where were the parents of the other children who dressed and acted this way? How involved were they and are they in these youngsters lives? Did no one see these kids as depressed? Did no one seek out help?

INVOLVEMENT

It is extremely difficult to become involved in your teenager's life if you have not been involved up to now. Teenagers as you know are seeking independence from their parents and families. It is part of the stage we call adolescence. They seek out an identity that allows them to separate from their parents as a way of making them more autonomous in their strife towards adulthood. The parent who has not gotten involved in their child's life before the teenage years begin will find this a very difficult proposition. The parent who has been involved all along will meet the challenge of staying involved with much greater ease. There are so many opportunities to be involved with your child. From the little league sports teams, to the boy/girl scouts, to the choir at church, the music lessons and the school plays and programs. Your child will present to you hundreds of opportunities to be involved in their life. They want you there. If your work schedule inhibits your involvement with your child, or your social life stops you from participating in their life, or your energies and attentions are pulling you in a different direction, then, you are telling your child that they are not important to you. Kids who get this message of unimportance at home, often get this message outside the home as well. These kids have not experienced success in the home, and they frequently will follow up with failure in social settings. The school is the child's main social arena!

Even though your teen is seeking independence from you, they are equally pulled towards interdependence with their peers. Peers take on such a significant role in the teen's development because the adolescent is trying to find out who they are outside the family. When kids do not feel successful in their lives at home, they seek out other kids who feel the same way about their homes. They unite with a common purpose. They fulfill the interdependence need with each other, and they feel a camaraderie because they believe that their peers truly understand them. Even though socially they are still quite inept, they gain comfort with each other by rallying against the more popular mainstream teen that has contributed to their "outcast" role at school. This is the likely scenario of the

Littleton, Colorado shooting. Two kids armed to the hilt seeking out athletes and minorities for vengeance.

Let's look at some clear warning signs for the troubled teenager:

◆ *Past history of violent and aggressive behavior* Unless there has been some successful intervention or on-going counseling, a youth who has a history of aggression towards others most likely will continue this type of behavior. The aggression may be directed toward others, or may be expressed in cruelty to animals or damage to property.

◆ *Drug use and alcohol use* As mentioned previously, this is a serious behavior that often accompanies destructive behavior. Self control and inhibitions are negatively affected with substance use. It also may indicate a lack of respect for the law, or feelings that the law does not apply to them.

◆ *Intolerance for differences and prejudicial attitudes* Displays of intense prejudice towards others often accompany the violent and aggressive teenager. Frequently, there is little or no censorship displayed about these feelings when he is angry. Sometimes the teen will join "hate" groups to foster the anger and prejudicial feelings. When parents see or hear the intolerance, they should act.

◆ *Affiliation with gangs* Not much different than the warning sign above. Gangs supporting anti-social values and behaviors and include intimidation tactics and acts of violence cause stress and fear in other students. Youth who are influenced by this type of anti-social behavior are giving us one of the clearest warning signs. Pay attention to this.

◆ *Inappropriate access to, possession of, and use of firearms* There is data supporting the increased risk for violence when children and youth are inappropriately exposed to firearms. There is also a higher risk for such youngsters becoming victims of shootings, stabbings, and physical violence.

◆ *Uncontrolled anger* Everyone gets angry. Anger that is expressed intensely and frequently in response to minor irritants may signal potential for violent behavior.

◆ *Low school interest and poor academic performance* Although the child may be intellectually bright, they usually do not get high grades. The idea that school is not a place where success occurs is a fairly common trait with the violent perpetrator of school assaults. Low school achievement may be caused by many factors. It is important to assess cognitive versus emotional challenges that contribute to poor performance.

◆ *Feelings of being picked on and persecuted* The youth who is teased, bullied and picked on is at high risk to deal with the ridicule in inappropriate ways. Often this child withdraws socially and isolates. Some children however may utilize aggression or violence as a way of expressing themselves.

◆ *Expression of violence in writings and drawings* Children and youth often express themselves through stories, or drawings. An over representation of violence in artwork or stories should be taken seriously. A professional counselor or psychologist should be considered. A number of violent teens have given warning signs first in their writings and drawings.

◆ *Being a victim of violence* Children who have experienced violence or abuse, sexual, or physical are at higher risk of perpetrating violence or abuse on others.

◆ *Patterns of impulsive and chronic hitting, intimidating and bullying behaviors* Similar to the past history of aggression warning signs, this one may be overlooked because the definition of aggression signifies more significant harm than the above behaviors. Kids who engage in these behaviors early in their childhood may be the child who ups the ante to more aggression later in their life.

Warning signs listed above taken from "A Guide to Safe Schools" pages 9-10. published by the Dept of Education, Washington D.C. 20202-2524

There are two kinds of mistakes parents can make when they read or see the warning signs listed above. The first mistake is that of denial. Those parents see a significant number of the signs in their child, but they deny the intensity and severity of the behaviors. They believe "My child is just going through a difficult phase, they will grow out of it", and then do nothing to intervene.

The next mistake would be the parent who sees one or two areas of concern in their child and believes that they are raising the next terrorist. There are some concerning behaviors listed in the warning signs above, but the parent must discern how long and intense the behavior in question has gone on. Is it an isolated incident, a single fight the teen has engaged in? Is it something that is chronic and causing much distress? Normal teenagers will display some of the behaviors listed above and they will learn from their mistakes. The concern should be heightened if there is a pattern of behavior or behaviors with your child.

If you are concerned about your teenager, talk to others. Network with school teachers, neighborhood parents, priests or ministers in your community, parents of your teen's friends, or professional counselors about your concern. The stakes are too high to do nothing. Your teenager's life, his happiness and the lives of others around him are simply too important.

Let's not forget that the disturbed teenager represents an extremely small percentage of our youth today. High schools today are filled with great kids. Hard working students who are both compassionate and loving fill 99.5% of the desks in our schools. These high energy youth are involved in part time jobs, sports teams, volunteer services in their communities, and church activities. They participate within their own families in healthy and productive ways. We should spend a little time talking about how to help the 99.5% with the senseless acts of violence that have infiltrated their lives.

First, let them talk about it. Teenagers need to talk about the feelings they are experiencing without judgment or comment about their feelings. Most teenagers will talk about it with their friends, but they also need permission to talk about it with their family. Many teens find it easier to express themselves when they are not at home. They report to me, that they would like to talk to mom or dad about their feelings, but they fear that mom and dad won't really listen. They are fearful that mom and dad will instead talk to them. The most valuable thing that you can do for your teenager who is trying to make sense out of this is to let him express himself. Encourage your son or daughter to write their feelings in a journal. Then express interest in their journals by asking permission to read them. Respect their decision if they do not want to share their journals.

Ask your teenager what you can do to help them. Many parents think they know what to do, and they neglect to get their teenager's suggestion.

Ask your teenager if they would like some other support. They may want to see a counselor, or get into an adolescent process group, or deal with another adult in their life to talk through their issues and feelings.

Discuss the warning signs in this chapter with your teen. Ask them if they are concerned about some of their peers as it relates to the warning symptoms. You may want to do this a couple of times with your teenager. Discussion of peers is often accompanied by a lot of defensiveness from the teenager. Assure them that your interest is not to isolate him from his peer group, but to address his feelings about safety.

Be aware of the symptoms that suggest that your child is not handling this stress well. If your child was directly exposed to the kind of trauma we are talking about, there is a strong possibility that he or she is experiencing a post traumatic stress response. Nightmares and flashbacks are often present for the person who directly experienced and survived the kind of assault and terror that has occurred in so many cities across our nation. Sleep and appetite disturbances and lethargy also accompany the depression that may be occurring with your child. Increased fear and insecurity are common with children affected by trauma. Your child did not have to be in the school to experience these emotional symptoms. If your child is having difficulty with any of the behaviors listed above, please get a professional psychologist and psychiatrist involved in his life.

What can Parents do to stop the madness? Earlier I emphasized the necessity of involvement in your child's life. I believe that through parental involvement, the child is able to find success and purpose. The child is able to realize that their parent is there to help whenever help is needed. The child develops strong roots in the family and then in society. Clearly, you need to make your child important. Do you need to have both parents in the workplace? If so, is that a need or a want? If you are too tired to interact with your child after your work day, then do it before you go into work.

Get involved with your child and their school. Be active in the curricula. Volunteer some time there so you can understand the place where your child spends half of his day. Coach a team, join the parent-teacher association. Ask the school for their needs, and then meet them.

Get involved. Do you know your neighbors? Do you know their kids? Spend time and get to know them. They are also parents with all the same demands that you have of yourselves. Make more of an effort than a superficial hello out at your mailbox.

Get involved. Meet your child's friends. Meet their parents too. Know more about them than a name. Establish effective communication with these people, it will pay off.

Get involved. Spend some special family time every week. Worship together, play together, work together.

If you simplify your lifestyle, you will find the time to get involved. And once you have gotten involved there is only one thing left to do: Stay Involved!!!

I want to complete this chapter by sharing with you a poem that my fourteen year old daughter wrote after the massacre at Columbine high school in Littleton, Colorado. This was the first time she has ever shared her writing with me. I am a proud father, and want to share it with you. It still touches me as I re-read it!

THE TRAGEDY
BY ERIN DIXON
April 21, 1999
FRESHMAN AT ST. MARY'S HIGH SCHOOL
COLORADO SPRINGS, COLORADO

I never knew you, I do not know your pain,
I've never seen your face, no one will ever see it again.
So sweet and innocent you left this place,
All who mourn you call it a waste.
For you to die so soon, so young,
You needed to do so much more, and have more fun!
You need to smile and laugh a lot,
Like you did before you were so needlessly shot.
But, up to Heaven you will go.
Leaving behind all you know.
Our prayers are for you, your family and friends,
Our sympathy for them never ends.
Someone's troubles took your life,
You were sacrificed to ease their strife.
Just like a rose that blooms before a frost,
Your life was frozen, and now, is lost.
Anger and sadness fill our hearts,
It feels like this pain will never depart.
Your Mama needs comfort, your Daddy too,
They just don't know how to cope without you.
So as you sit there, up above.
Remember all who felt your love.

Dedicated to all the students who died in the tragedy at
Columbine High School and all the other senseless killings
in our nation's schools.

CHAPTER TEN

Your Teenager as a Co-Parent

IN CHAPTER TEN YOU WILL FIND

- Engaging your teen in the process of limit setting and contracting
- Building in positive incentives and rewards
- Knowing your role in the power struggles that occur and avoiding them
- Getting your child to set limits on their own behaviors

Behavioral contracting with your teenager is not a new idea. The emphasis of this book has been on making sure that the parents are able to behave in a consistent and reliable way when dealing with their children. As mentioned in an earlier chapter, when teens reach the ages sixteen and seventeen, they are developmentally in a really good position to negotiate. If you are able to engage this older teen in the process of limit-setting, your job as a parent is made a hundred times easier. You do not have to wait for your teenager to turn sixteen to begin getting him or her involved in the parenting process. It makes a lot of sense to sit down with your adolescent (even if they are only twelve or thirteen) to discuss reasonable limits on their behavior. You might approach it in this way: "Your mother and I are concerned about your recent problems in school. We are discussing the idea of putting more structure over your home time to help you out with your schooling. What do you think is reasonable?" If your teen resists the notion of having any changes made (e.g., saying things like, "I'll get my grades up, just get off my back"). He or she is telling you that he or she is not mature enough in this matter to set appropriate limits on the particular behavior. Teenagers in this position are telling you that they are not able to help you with your parenting decisions, and, in effect, they are asking you to make all of the decisions for them. I often recommend that parents tell teenagers that this is the message the teens are conveying. Sometimes the teenager is able to regroup later and to begin to share in the dialogue around limits. This is much more likely to take place if the parents are able to tie in this conversation with the notion of maturity. Teenagers, like adults, hate the notion that they are not behaving in mature ways. The notion of immaturity attacks their developmental drive for independence, but if the reintroduction of this idea is handled in a tactful way, it may make them respond in less emotional ways.

Even though the bulk of this book is about empowering parents to remove privileges when their children choose negative behaviors, the most successful parent is not merely restricting things of importance for their child. Setting up positive incentives as rewards is also vitally important. Obviously, teens are happier when they do not have their privileges restricted, but this is not all the parent can do as far as providing incentives for their adolescent. An unemotional parent learns to negotiate with a teenager over his or her needs and wants, and to work those needs and wants into the behavioral contract as positive incentives. Most teenagers striving for independence and adulthood want privileges that push the limits of their chronological and developmental ages. Fourteen to fifteen year old girls may want to date, the sixteen year old boy may want no curfew on the weekends, and thirteen year old teens may want to be able to watch R-rated movies. Drinking, smoking, and sexual behavior are viewed by teenagers as rites of passage into adulthood, and adolescents begin experimenting with these behaviors as ways of pushing the limits of their own age. Peers tend to have tremendous influence as far as behaviors go, and teens who have friends who drink or smoke, for example, are highly likely to be engaging in these behaviors themselves.

The parents who are trying to get their teenagers to participate in their own parenting, and who are trying to bring the teen into the limit-setting and structure-building discussions, may have a hard time setting up some of the "adult" behaviors described above as incentives. Compromise is your most valuable tool in this situation. For example, a fourteen or fifteen year old girl may want to date, and the rules of the home might be that dating can begin at age sixteen. If you are addressing a school performance problem, and you are trying to set more restrictive limits on home time to help this girl get her grades up, how do you figure in the incentive of dating? You may reward the fifteen year old for complying with the structure (e.g., coming home for dinner at 5:30 p.m., studying between 6:00 p.m. and 8:00 p.m., enjoying telephone time and free time at home from 8:00 to 9:30, and being in bed by 10:00) by allowing her to go out on group dates one weekend night if they have been properly planned out. These group dates allow the fifteen year old to test the dating game in a safer situation, and they also allow them to be viewed by their friends as okay. This is a good compromise to present to the kid who is demanding to date. You have built in a very important incentive for your teen, and you have increased the odds of her responding positively to the limits around her schoolwork that you have placed in her life.

The notion of getting your kid involved in the contracting and limit-setting applies to kids of all ages, and the notion of building in positive incentives does so as well. Remember the nine year old who earned a candy bar for getting to bed without arguing and struggling, and then was able to turn in twenty five candy bar wrappers for a pizza party or an NBA basketball game? This is a good example of parents building in a positive incentive for displaying positive behavior.

I often ask adolescents how they would respond to a particular problem if they were the parents, in an attempt to discover how they think about the problem. I ask questions like, "What do you think is a fair consequence, given that you were told to do such and such, and you still decided to do things your own way?" Or "What do you think is a fair way to set consequences on you when you break your curfew?" These types of questions usually get better responses and more participation if you remove yourself from the heat of the battle. The best way do that is to discuss the problem, and get your child's input at a time when the problem is not occurring. By allowing time to pass between the problem's occurrence and the discussion of the consequences makes all involved better able to discuss the matter in a less emotional way, and the results are usually more productive. For example, you may pick a Saturday afternoon during a family drive or activity to initiate a discussion about a problem with school that you are trying to correct. If you ask your son or daughter their ideas about how you can be a better parent around helping them get their schoolwork turned in on time during a non-threatening time they will probably be able to openly discuss the problem. They will respond with less defensiveness and less minimization than they would if you approached this topic immediately after getting a poor report card. When children perceive that their parents are not upset, but rather are rational and unemotional, they participate in discussions in more mature ways themselves. Asking a teenager, "What would you do if you were the parent?" often yields a great deal of insight into how severe they perceive the particular problem to be.

You will do well to remember that your teens want to be more in control of their lives, and that they view parents and other authority figures as intrusive. If you are able to use this notion to your advantage, you may be able to get them to set appropriate limits on themselves. When kids are able to place limits on their own behavior, they will have come a long way towards maturation. Reminding the teen that they want less parental involvement in their lives by saying things to them such as, "I know that you want us to back off, but when you choose to behave like you are, you are telling us that you really need us more involved in your life." or, " We are going to set limits on your behavior if you make choices that require our involvement," are subtle but effective ways of pushing your teenager to set limits on their own behaviors.

Comments such as "We want to tell you some of the consequences that we have come up with to address these problems, and we want your input on these consequences". or, "We are willing to listen to your thoughts on how we should address these problem behaviors". or, "If you can begin to make better choices then you will be allowed to have what you want. We will be less involved in your life, and we will be willing to look at increasing your privileges". "You have to show us that you are able to make more mature choices and get these problems taken care of, if you want us to set less restrictions on you." Are all excellent ways of talking to your older teenager and promoting personal responsibility within them. You need to get you teens involved in two ways. First, you need to ask them for input regarding the appropriate consequences for their problem behaviors; then, you need to build in incentives that they can gain for themselves by making more mature and responsible choices. In this process, you are making them responsible for the choices they make, and you are talking to them in ways that are consistent with their developmental stage.

CHAPTER ELEVEN

Let's Talk About Talk

IN CHAPTER ELEVEN YOU WILL FIND

- Reviewing the internal struggles that characterize the adolescent period:
  - separating from parents
  - seeking their own identity
  - resisting authority
  - externalizing blame outside of self
- Effective language parents can use that is consistent with the unemotional parenting philosophy
- The parental notion of control
- Language that puts the child in charge of their own choices
- Helping parents to talk to each other and to present themselves to their kids as a team
- Predicting your teen's behavior, a paradoxical and effective strategy

The way you talk to your children is very important. Unemotional parenting is about understanding the developmental stages and developmental needs of your children so that you may be the most effective parent. Your ability to effectively communicate with your teenager is also dependent on your understanding of his or her developmental stage. One of the greatest changes that adolescents experience is the beginning of their separation from their parents, and one of their goals is to tell the parents in direct and indirect ways that they are not them. Understanding this developmental issue will help direct you in the way(s) that you talk with your teen. Remember your own adolescence. What kinds of things did you do to tell your own parents that you were part of a new generation, and not a member of theirs? When I was entering adolescence, the Beatles were making their way onto the American scene. They came with long hair, and they wrote and sang music that drove my parents crazy. They were clearly nothing like Bing Crosby, Perry Como, or Frank Sinatra. Playing the Beatles on my record player was one way that I was saying that I was not either of my parents. Later in my adolescence I began wearing my hair longer, and I started wearing clothes that were not to my parents liking. I began arguing with my dad over who was the greater heavyweight champion, Muhammad Ali, or, his favorite, Rocky Marciano. I told him that Gayle Sayers could run circles around his favorite running back, and we had many arguments comparing the athletes of my generation to the athletes of his. These are very normal generational struggles. Even though I have cautioned you against using your own adolescence as a frame of reference for understanding your teen (because of the dramatic social changes that have taken place), it is important to realize that the internal struggles facing your teen are very similar to those you faced when you were a teenager. For example, no adult generation likes the music of the upcoming teen generation, nor do they like the hairstyles or the dress. Today, kids listen to heavy metal music, or gangster rap, or alternative music, and most parents do not share their teen's liking for these types of music. Kids today are also shaving their heads on one side, wearing rings in their noses and ears, and tattooing their shoulders, wrists, and other body parts. These are some of the ways the teenagers of today are telling the adult generation that they are different.

Another central struggle in the adolescent developmental stage is about resisting authority. Parents are still the ultimate authority, and their adolescents find ways to struggle with them and their rules. These conflicts reach their peak intensity during this time in the child's life. Adolescents are striving at this point for independence and adulthood. They, like us, want to be the authors of their own thoughts, and they want to be in the position of making their own rules. They resist anyone telling them what to do because this conflicts with the notion that they are capable of doing things on their own. They believe that they know what is best for themselves, and they often will argue with you on any issue where you are discussing their welfare. For example, if you enter a discussion with a pot-smoking adolescent about the negative effects of marijuana, you will get a strong and emotional response telling you that marijuana has no ill effects. For every point that you make, he or she will tell of a friend or acquaintance who uses pot and does not experience that difficulty. Chemical-dependency experts call this "denial." Within adolescence lies a resistance to the idea that anyone besides themselves can possibly know what is good for them. They simply do not want to be told what to do.

Despite wanting to be in control of their own behaviors and their own thought processes, adolescents are masters at externalizing. This means that they will often refuse to acknowledge personal responsibility for the problems in their lives. They blame their bad grades in algebra on their teacher, telling you that no one can do well with that teacher. They come home late at night and tell you that the friend who was driving would not take them home when they asked. Or, they rationalize, that the 7-11 store asks for people to steal their goods by raising their prices, and everyone does it! These are all examples of teenagers externalizing responsibility. Externalizing depends largely on maturity, and some teens are able to accept personal responsibility better than others. You have a very immature adolescent if you begin to apply unemotional parenting techniques, and the teenager insists that the problem lies within the consequence that you set, rather than the choice that they made. When this happens, you need to know how to talk to your teenager so that they can hear you, and eventually be able to take personal responsibility for their own choices.

In unemotional parenting you actually put the teenager in charge of their behavior and their choices. Those teens who choose a negative course of action (e.g., not doing their chores) and then blame the parent for the consequence that follows require a different approach from you than they have been receiving. Most likely, they have been receiving arguments and lectures from you. The unemotional parenting approach is different and more effective. As parents we need to avoid certain responses, and we need to let go of the notion that we can control our child. In unemotional parenting we are putting the child in total control of his or her behaviors. Developmentally, this is what they are striving for, and this striving is the cause of most of the oppositional behavior we see from this age group. As I've stated earlier, we must make it hard for our child to choose a negative or dangerous course of action, but they are ultimately in charge of their own choices. In effect, when your kids enter into pre-teen years, you must quit telling them what to do, and instead establish appropriate consequences that will help them decide the appropriate course of action. When you do this successfully, you will be helping to raise a teenager who is able to accept personal responsibility for their own choices. When you understand this concept of control, you will reduce your power struggles with your kids a thousandfold. Your children are responsible for the choices they make, and you are responsible for following through with the appropriate consequences.

In Chapter Two, I began discussing how parents need to talk to their kids. I would like to spend some time here discussing that issue. When kids learn that their parents communicate effectively with each other they realize that they are dealing with a consistent team approach to their problems, requests, and behaviors. So, in short, before you will be effective in your communication with your child, you must be successful communicating with each other. One of the most common mistakes that well-intended parents make is when one of them responds to the child's request in a favorable way, and then adds that it is only O.K. if the other parent agrees. For example, mom might say, "Yes, you can have the car this weekend, if you check it out with your dad first." The reason that this sets up problems should be obvious to you. First, it disrupts the communication between parents and places the kid in the middle of the communication process. The kid should not have to check with his or her dad (or mom) after he or she makes a request. The parents should be talking *together* about the child's request. The next problem that occurs has been discussed at length in Chapter Two, i.e., that being the problem of the parenting team splitting into a team where one is perceived as "easy" and the other as the "harsher" parent. Consistent parenting is much more difficult once this process has begun. You child should grow used to hearing, "We will talk about it and let you know" when they make a request from one of you.

The major point here is that your kid must view you as a parenting team. He or she will benefit tremendously from your teamwork, and the power struggles will occur less frequently when you are communication with each other effectively and often. Talk as though you are a team (i.e., as "we" not "I") when you are responding to their requests and setting limits on their behaviors.

Single parents who can not utilize this teamwork approach can delay their responses to their child's request. Discussing parenting with support persons such as grandparents, neighborhood adults, counselors, and other parents of teenagers will help the single parent who is without a parenting partner make appropriate and effective decisions.

I stated that effective communication with your children begins with effective communication with yourselves. Even with our best parenting efforts, we do not agree on everything. It is sometimes necessary to find a place in your home to discuss your differences away from your children, so that you may work out your differences, reach a compromise, and then present yourselves to your children in a unified way. Compromise is an important tool that parents need to utilize when they disagree. A good strategy would be for the parent who compromised their position to be the spokesperson to the kid concerning the issue in question. For example, the fourteen year old daughter wants to go to a concert. Mom is okay with the request, but Dad is not. After they have discussed this issue together, Dad agrees to give in and let the daughter attend the concert. It works best if Dad is able to then tell his daughter that "We have decided that it is okay for you to go to the concert." Similarly, if Mom compromised to Dad's position, and the daughter was not going to be allowed to go to the concert, she should be the spokesperson who says, "We have decided that you are not going to go to the concert, and here is why...". When this occurs, in this way, the daughter does not know who is "soft" and who is "hard" because both parents are playing both roles. Parents, I suggest to you that you take turns being the bearer of good news and the bearer of bad news for your children for exactly this reason. A parenting team that I worked with utilized a poker chip to help them to compromise. One parent held the poker chip, and when a dispute presented itself with the other parent, the one with the poker chip "won" the dispute. Of course, in winning the dispute the parent had to turn the poker chip over to the other parent so that the next disagreement would go their way. This was a delightful way of handling differences. It lightened up the emotionality attached to mom and dad's position on any given topic, and it kept the teamwork approach intact for the children who never knew about the way that mom and dad made the decisions around their requests.

The way you communicate with your children is vitally important to unemotional parenting. Unemotional parenting stresses that you as parents understand the developmental phases and struggles that your children are going through. The way you talk to them reflects that understanding, and increases your chances of success as parents. When you are able to talk to your kid about the choices they have made, and empower him or her in making more appropriate choices, then you will also be able to let go of some of the controls that you have been holding onto. Parents gradually lose their controls over the different areas of a child's life as he or she grows older, and this is one of the reasons that parenting can become so frustrating. They need to empower their kids by telling them that their behaviors are choices that they are making and then hold them accountable for making both correct and incorrect choices. It is quite all right to tell your kids that you know that you cannot control them or their choices. You are reinforcing the idea that they are in control of their own lives, and responsible for the consequences that follow their choices. When you outline a consequence for your teenager, say something like this: "If you are unable to maintain your grades above a C average, then you will be choosing to enroll in summer school this summer." Make sure that you include in your statement that they are choosing these consequences. These are the operative words to use in empowering teenagers to make good decisions and feel ultimately responsible for any behavior that they display.

The next part of this kind of communication comes when your child does choose a negative course of action. As a parent, you may be extremely tempted to lecture your child about his or her choice. You may want to tell your kid how important an education is when he or she has just brought home four Ds and two F's. You may want to tell them how hard you worked on your studies, and how it paid off in the end. You may want to lecture them about the negative peer group that they are hanging around with, and tell them that their friends are impacting their grades. None of this is very useful. By the time your kids reach adolescence they understand most, if not all, of your values. They have heard your lectures on each of the important issues in their lives. They know that you value education, that you want them to respect adults, that curfews are set for a reason, and that they must put their own needs ahead of the needs of their friends. They have heard your lectures, and even though most parents can't resist repeating them every time their kid violates a rule, the lecturing mode is usually quite ineffective with teenagers. Most children tune their parents out, or roll their eyes in pain at the lecture that follows a problem behavior.

Unemotional parenting makes the limit-setting part of parenting much easier. Your job is largely done in the above incident after you have said, "I wonder why you chose to go to summer school in June, instead of playing pony league baseball." You are following through with a consequence that the kid had known would come if he or she did not get their grades up. Of course, various arguments and a fair amount of complaining will likely follow from your teen when they realize that you are going to follow through with your end of the contract. You can even use unemotional parenting to deal with this kind of verbal behavior by talking to your kids about the choices they have made. The limits you set up are not about what *you* are doing; they are about your role in what *they* are doing!

Your kids do know your values, but they cannot be force-fed values in their teenage years. Hopefully, over the course of the first ten to twelve years of life, they have gained a pretty good understanding of what is important to you. In adolescence, testing values and experimenting with consequences are normal processes. Adolescents are trying to find their own identity, and sometimes this requires breaking the rules around the values that they have learned. Oftentimes, lecturing them on the rightness or wrongness of an act makes them dig in even more, because they are striving to be independent from you.

In an earlier portion of this book, I talked about the importance of doing things as a family. Often, teens who seek out their own activities for leisure lose touch with the enjoyable parts of belonging to a family. They describe their parents as "hounds", always nagging them or lecturing them about something. They often view their parents in a negative way, and the balancing of enjoying each other's company while setting limits on negative behaviors is often difficult to keep. Your kids will hear your criticisms and negative feedback much better if you are able to counter balance them with positives, by making it fun and enjoyable to be a part of the family. This counter balancing makes unemotional parenting much easier. Find some time to stay involved with your kids, even when they are seemingly pushing you away to be with their peers. Build in time during the week to have light and enjoyable contact with each other. Parenting does not always have to be a power struggle, and your ability to play together will make it less of one.

When you are spending quality fun time with your pre-teen or teenager, try to remove yourself from the role of expert. It makes sense to make your kid the expert on some things, and if you allow them to teach you things about themselves, you will enhance your relationship with them. For example, if you watch a movie that has a difficult theme, such as teenage pregnancy, drug use, suicide, or gang violence, you do not need to be the teacher. It is often tempting for parents to use such movies as springboards into lectures with their own teenagers, but you may achieve much more if you put your teenager in charge of the discussion, and make them the expert on some of these topics. If you ask them open ended questions like, "What did you think of that movie?" or "Do those things happen at your high school?" or if you make non-threatening comments like, "Boy, when I was a teenager, I did not have to worry about my friends wanting to kill themselves: is that really the way it is these days?" your kid will be encouraged to discuss these things with you. Respect your kid, and encourage them to talk about the serious issues in their lives, while avoiding "Right vs Wrong" lectures. Show interest in them by allowing them to discuss these difficult subjects without worrying that they might be judged harshly for their responses. If you begin moving into the role of a coach, you will find that your parenting role will get easier. A coach is often able to teach a protégé without the protégé becoming defensive, and the protégé is able to learn in this way.

Let's move on with some other strategies that come into play in talking to your child. One successful approach to talking with adolescents involves subtle comments about their maturity. An overly critical parent will not be able to pull this off, but the parent who has a good balance in their relationship with their teen may often refer to the teenager's choices as a reflection of his or her maturity. Remember the example of the parents who placed significant after-school structures on their teenage daughter because she chose to allow her grades to go in the toilet? They basically told her that they would remove their structures when she showed that she was mature enough to do without them. Frequently, in my private practice I have been able to use suggestions of immaturity to my advantage. I had a fifteen year old once who was chronically truant from school. When his mother brought him to see me, I conducted an interview that I called "A developmental assessment." At the end of the hour I told the youngster that he needed to continue skipping school, because he had missed a very important developmental phase that most boys go through when they are ten. I told him that his parents had to be to blame, because at age ten he should have already gone through the phase of hating school and wanting to play all the time. I told him to keep missing school, so that he could catch up in maturity with his peers. I told his mom that if he did not miss school now, he might never mature to the level of normal fifteen year olds. Furthermore, I told him that he would know he had reached the maturity of other fifteen year olds when he no longer desired to ditch school. At this time he would look forward to seeing how well he could perform at school, as a way of competing with his same-aged mates, and preparing himself for his adult life.

Obviously, this young man hated the notion that his behavior was immature, and that I had said he was struggling with an issue that most people struggle with at age ten. I, however, was the expert who had been sought out for a professional assessment of the problem. When I told him to keep ditching school until he had successfully gotten past his immaturity, he did not know what to think. He went back to school on his own volition the next day. Even though, I emphasized in our next session that he was rushing through a very important developmental struggle, he insisted that he really wanted to get back to school. In this incident, I utilized the teen's desire to be more mature and grown-up. I am not suggesting that all parents can use reverse psychology techniques to "manipulate" their teen's behavior, but I am prompting you to be aware of the strong developmental issues that your teen is struggling with. From time to time, you may be able to talk to your teen successfully about his or her mature or immature choices.

The risk of "reverse psychology" techniques like the one I just described is obvious. Imagine if the teenager took my suggestion to miss more school in a different way. If he chose to continuing missing school, he would have an excellent excuse. His parents would have had a truant fifteen year old who basically received permission from an "expert" to continue his problem behaviors. Since I am talking about paradoxes, I can't resist telling you a story about a time when this technique backfired on me. Fortunately this "reverse psychology" trial occurred with a three year old and not a fifteen year old. Fortunately the consequences for the failed trial were not too severe. Reverse psychology often works well with children around the age of three. These children are struggling with a miniature version of independence-seeking. With most three year olds, all you have to do to have them pick up after themselves is tell them that they are not big enough to do so. "You are only three; you are not big enough to pick up your toys, so I will do it." They often say, "I am so big enough." To which you playfully respond, "Nah, you are only three, you are still a baby." Sure enough, they will try to prove you wrong, and you will end up congratulating them on being such a big boy or girl. Well, it doesn't always work that way. I had a three year old boy named Ronnie come into my office one day. He made a shambles of the waiting room while I spoke to his mother. He threw magazines everywhere, and began to color on my new wallpaper. I thought I would impress the mom by showing her just how well I understood kids. I said, "Ronnie, you are making a mess in my office. How old are you?" He shyly answered, "three". I continued, "Oh, you are just a little boy, then. You are too little to pick up the mess you made; I will have to pick it up." He said, "I told you, mom, I am too little to be doing work." Mom smiled and shrugged her shoulders, and they left. I learned right then and there that reverse psychology carries some risks. It does not work all the time, and when it does not you may end up with egg on your face (or, in this case, crayon on your walls).

Another way of talking to your teenagers, and a strategy that pays off consistently, is the strategy of predicting your teen's behavior in conversation with him or her. This works well even with young adults. When you tell people how they are going to respond, it almost guarantees that they will not respond in that way. No one likes to think that others know them so well that they can predict their reaction to a given situation or stimulus. You might say, "You are not going to like what I have to say. You will probably get angry and leave before we are finished discussing this, but I still need to talk to you." Nine times out of ten, if you preface your remark with a prediction of how your listener will react (i.e., "You will probably get angry and leave before we are finished discussing this"), you will insure that the person will not react this way. You might say, "I know that I cannot make you come home by 10:30 p.m., and that you will choose to stay out after this curfew, but you need to know what consequences are going to go along with that choice. If you choose to stay out after curfew, you will lose your car the following weekend." In this example, you are admitting to your teen that you are not in control of their behavior, and you are predicting the behavior that they will display. Finally, you are informing them of the consequences for choosing this negative course of action. All of these messages hold true with the principles of unemotional parenting.

You may want to predict your teen's behaviors after they break one of your rules, This kind of prediction may sound like this: "I know that you're going to be upset, and I'm sure that you will end up cussing me out, but I am following through on the consequence that you chose. You will not get your car this weekend because you chose to stay out until 11:45 p.m. last night." In this example, you are trying to stop additional arguments, excuse-making, and swearing by predicting that your teen will respond in this way. You may even want to use prediction in a more subtle way. As you describe the behaviors that you want your teenager to modify, you may say,

"I'm not expecting you to be able to come around and begin following the rules of this house. I don't know if it is a maturity issue or what, but you have not been able to set any limits on your own behavior. That is why I am going to let you know what the consequences are going to be if you choose to continue acting this way. I don't like setting limits on you, but until you show that you are mature enough to make good choices, I will keep setting them." This way of communicating subtly predicts the teen's behaviors by way of the suggestion of immaturity.

You may also use predictions as reminders of the limits that have been set up. For instance, you may predict to your middle-aged adolescent on Monday or Tuesday that he or she probably is not going to catch up on all of the missed homework assignments that he or she has and be free to go to a concert on Saturday. This example assumes that you have told your teenager that he or she must catch up on school work before going out to see his or her favorite heavy metal band that weekend. When you see the teen procrastinating and spending his or her free time unwisely on Monday or Tuesday, you may use this kind of prediction as a motivation. It helps you out as well, doesn't it? If your kid becomes motivated in order to show you that you are wrong, and he or she gets to the school work, you benefit. Your kid is finishing school and you have avoided a huge power struggle on the day of the concert that certainly would have come up if he or she had chosen to let their homework slide. Even though you are practicing unemotional parenting, your kids will not make your job easy. Your resolve will be tested many times as in the situation described above. If your child does not get the homework done, the day of that important concert will come and your kid will begin to try to convince you why you need to back off from the limit you have set. The teenager will hope to convince you that your limit is the problem, not the choices that he or she made that required that limit. Every time that you pass the tests that they give you as parents (i.e., by continuing to apply unemotional parenting, and talking to your children about **their** responsibility and **their** choices), you are making future tests easier to pass. Your kids will start to learn that you are not going back to your emotional parenting style, in which tests were constantly given by them and seldom passed by you. How you talk to your kids goes a long way towards reaching the parent-child relationship that you want.

In conclusion, let's walk through a contrast of emotional and unemotional parenting, so that you can see how very easy it is to make these changes, and how the end results are dramatically different.

REQUEST FROM TEEN: "Mom, there is no school tomorrow. It is a teacher planning day. I want to go out with some friends tonight! Can I?"

EMOTIONAL	UNEMOTIONAL
MOM: It is O.K., but I want you home by 11:00 p.m. Don't you be late!	MOM: Let me talk this over with dad and we will get back to you. (later) We have decided it is O.K. for you to go, but we also need you to be home by 11:00 p.m. If you come home after 11:00 p.m., you will lose your weekend.

TEEN comes home at 12:30 a.m., an hour and a half after the time requested.

MOM: I told you to be home at 11:00 p.m. I have been worried sick. You are almost two hours late. YOU ARE GROUNDED FOR A MONTH, AND YOU CAN'T HAVE THE CAR FOR THE NEXT THREE WEEKS. NOW GET TO BED!	MOM: It is past midnight. I wonder why you chose to lose your weekend. Friday and Saturday you will stay home. Now get to bed!

TEEN: Wait a minute, it wasn't even my fault that I'm late. It is not fair for you to ground me. I told Jordan that I needed to go home, but he was in the middle of a blowout with his girlfriend. He didn't get around to taking me home until 12:15 a.m.

MOM: I told you that I don't even want you hanging around Jordan. He is always getting into trouble.

TEEN: You hate all my friends. Jordan is cool; what is wrong with him?

MOM: He dropped out of school, he smokes pot, and he cusses me out on the phone when he calls. He is a loser. Why don't you hang around with Steve any more?

TEEN: As a matter of fact, Steve just asked me to go to the lake with him and his family this weekend. He is still my friend. Is that O.K.?

MOM: Is Jordan going?

Nah, Steve and Jordan don't like each other. Can I go?

MOM: I guess so.

MOM: I know that you are not going to like this conversation. I think that you will probably get angry and storm off on me but I am going to stick to my guns on your consequence. You know the rules on curfew. It was your decision to rely on Jordan for a ride. You know how unreliable he is.

TEEN: I can't believe that you are still grounding me for Friday and Saturday? It wasn't my fault.

MOM: I think that you need to think about your choices, and think about your relationship with Jordan. The consequence sticks. Next time get home on time!

TEEN: But this weekend I wanted to go to the lake with Steve and his family.

MOM: I wonder why you chose to miss that. I like Steve a lot. You'll have to tell him that you can't go this weekend.

It is easy to see the differences in the two approaches. With the emotional response the teen was able to deflect the discussion to the subject of his friends. The emotional parent got sidetracked by a more heated subject, his friend Jordan, and the teen quickly lost the consequences that she had put on him just a few moments earlier. The unemotional parent, however, kept the focus on the curfew, and on the child's responsibility to keep it. She utilized "prediction" to insure that the conversation would reach a conclusion (i.e., predicting that her son would get mad and storm out of the room increased the probability that he would not respond that way). She addressed the friend issue, but only briefly and in a way that made her son responsible for his choice of friends.

CHAPTER TWELVE

The Great Equalizer

IN CHAPTER TWELVE YOU WILL FIND

- How children make their parents re-evaluate their responses
  - running away from home
  - suicide ideation or attempts
  - drug and alcohol abuse
- Using community resources and other support systems to assist you in dealing with your child's dangerous behavior

One of the great equalizers that adolescents have is to behave in dangerous and threatening ways. Many parents have teenagers who have used running away, suicidal threats and behaviors and drug and alcohol abuse as ways of responding to conflicts and stress in their lives, and these parents know how very scary these things are. These types of behaviors make parents re-evaluate their responses and try new parenting techniques to deal with their kids. When these types of behaviors present themselves, parents turn into emotional reactors. They see their child's life as being at risk, and no one can stay unemotional under these circumstances. Some parents back off of their parenting responsibilities after their children engage in this kind of behavior. I worked with a mother whose fifteen year old son Ben, was heavily into marijuana and other substances. The mother placed her son in drug and alcohol treatment for a period of about seven months. When Ben returned to her home, she became ineffective in dealing with him because of her fear that he may again start using drugs. He would ask if he could go to a friend's house on a Friday night. Mother would allow this, and she would ask Ben to be home by midnight. Ben would end up calling Mom at around 11:55 p.m. and report that he and his friend were wanting to watch a movie. He would ask for permission to stay longer. Every time she would allow him to stay for his movie (even if it were a three hour long movie), as long as Ben checked in with her before his prescribed curfew. When I asked mother why she was so willing to back off on the time that Ben should return home, she stated, "I think he has come a long way from doing the drugs. I would rather allow him to stay at a friend's than have him hanging with his old drug group!" In this case, mother became very soft around her limits. As long as Ben stayed away from the marijuana he was allowed to do other behaviors that were not age appropriate. Mother's fear of a return to the earlier problem stopped her from applying appropriate limits with her son. Sadly, Ben returned to the marijuana problem as well. When she tried to pull him back by initiating strong limits once again, Ben responded with aggression and anger. Once again he required an out of home placement.

Parents who begin utilizing unemotional parenting may get one of the scary responses described in this chapter from their kids in the hopes that the parent will revert back to their old parenting style. How are the parents to respond?

I was working with a parenting team once who felt completely helpless and powerless in dealing with their fourteen year old daughter, Emily. Since age thirteen, this attractive young lady had been disappearing from home whenever her parents had tried to exercise controls and limits on her. She had been utilizing a network of friends, and moving from one friend's home to the next every three to five days. All the while, the parents would worry frantically about Emily's whereabouts and her safety. When she would return home (usually after having set up her own capture by her parents) the parents would back off from their limits and rules. They would be so happy to see their daughter safe and to have her back home that there would literally be no consequence placed on her for running away. In fact, Emily would actually be reinforced for running away since in a sense it would get her what she wanted. This situation soon reached the point that when I suggested appropriate consequences for any one of the negative behaviors that Emily displayed, the dad would respond, "No, I can't do that. She will hit the road again."

After several sessions, I was able to help the parents understand that their daughter was showing a need for more and not less structure and limits in her life by displaying these behaviors. When they began to see this need, they were soon able to give appropriate parenting responses to their child's behavior. They began utilizing public support systems to help them with this very scary and difficult problem. They contacted the local police, and found out how to respond when Emily disappeared. Next, they contacted the school that Emily attended and got a list of her friends and their telephone numbers. The parents also utilized me, a licensed clinical psychologist and a family therapist, to help them deal appropriately with the problem. With my assistance, the parents got in touch with an adolescent psychiatric hospital unit.

Here is what happened: The parents admitted to Emily that they could not stop her from running away. They let her know how scary this was for them, but they told her that the knew that she could still run away in spite of their objections and fears. They told her that if she chose to run away again, they would contact the police and file a runaway report. They told Emily that the police usually required a 24-hour wait before accepting a report, but that in her case they would take the report anytime it was filed. They told Emily that the police would have a list of her friends, and that they would begin looking for her. They also told her that the parents of her known friends had been instructed to contact either them or the police if she showed up. They also told Emily that when the police found her, they would take her to the adolescent psychiatric hospital that served their community. Finally, they told her that if she chose to run away again, she would lose two important things when she returned home. She would lose her own room, and would have to share a room with her youngest sister for four months. If she went four months without running away, and she complied to the house rules, she would earn her own room back. The other thing Emily would lose would be her ability to come and go as she pleased. She would need to check in after school, and get permission before going out with her friends. This was a new requirement place on Emily. Prior to this, Emily was pretty much able to come and go as she pleased.

Do you see how these responses were consistent with unemotional parenting? The parents had been made to feel totally powerless in their situation, but by applying the principles of this approach they were able to completely reverse their situation. Emily did run away again - three more times. Each time, she was found within 48 hours of leaving. Each time, the parents with help from their support systems, dealt with her behaviors appropriately. She gradually learned that running away caused her more problems than she was willing to take on. She hated the police hassling her friends' parents, she hated going to the psychiatric hospital, and she hated losing privileges that meant something to her every time she returned to her family. Emily is now almost seventeen years old, and she has not run away for three years.

Many parents who have runaway teens neglect to apply a concrete negative consequence to their behavior when they return home. Common sense dictates that consequences should be applied upon the return. If I were to run away for three to five days, many consequences would be waiting for me when I returned. I would most likely lose my job, because my supervisor would not be nearly so thrilled to see my safe return. I would also lose the income that went with my job. I would probably lose my wife, because she would assume all sorts of unsavory motives and behaviors behind my disappearance without her knowledge. I would lose my house in the divorce, and I would have to find a new residence. The point is that there are significant consequences for such drastic behaviors. Your teenagers should not escape the natural consequences that follow their running away adventure. Again, if you have a child who chronically runs away, like Emily above, your task is to inform your kid about the consequences before he or she does this again. Then you are talking to your children about the choices they are making, and not reacting emotionally in the eleventh hour. This is the heart of unemotional parenting.

When kids utilize suicidal gestures or suicidal ideas as ways of dealing with the stress in their lives, parents need to get outside help. Do not start guessing about how serious your kid is in this kind of thinking. A professional mental health evaluation and possibly hospitalization may be called for. You do not control your teen's emotions or behaviors, and you are not responsible for his or her reactions or choices. In these scary times you need to realize that your most effective parenting tool will be to get other support systems involved in your family.

When adolescents get in over their head in drug or alcohol abuse, the same advice applies. You might need professional support to help you with a problem this large. Adolescence is a stage where a person's emotions fluctuate and change like the wind, and if your teens are partying and using chemicals in order to feel good about themselves they will experience exaggerated and sometimes dangerous mood swings that will affect your whole family.

Feelings of helplessness and powerlessness are related to the erroneous notion that some parents have that they are all alone in the task of rearing their children. Help for parents can take on many forms. How many of you have utilized the teachers at your kid's school, the coaches of your child's sport teams, the neighborhood adults that your kid has befriended, or the members of your local church? Grandparents, uncles, aunts and other family members are also frequently untapped support systems. Adolescents have a strange way of relating to adults. More often than not, they will vehemently oppose their parents at home but respond quite positively to other adults in their world. As parents, we need to recognize that our teens can learn many lessons from other adults and that hooking the teacher that they really like, or the coach that they work extremely hard for, may help you a lot in your home.

In most communities, mental health centers provide more than individual or family counseling services. Often they offer seminars and courses on topics like teenage stresses, reducing anger in the family, and the effects of drugs and alcohol on the family. Many parents believe that the Department of Social Services (DSS) only exists to police and punish parents for abusive or neglectful parenting, but it can also be a valuable source of help in circumstances that have gone out of control. Most communities have 12-step support groups that address alcohol and drug involvement and addiction. These groups are invaluable sources of information about chemical dependency and abuse. Alanon, Coda, Alateen, AA, CA, and NA are all groups that can support you in the difficult area of addiction. Many communities also have parenting support groups like Tough Love and P.E.T. (Parent Effectiveness Training). These groups are often comprised of other parents who are experiencing difficulties similar to your own. Networking with other parents can be an extremely valuable resource for you.

A major idea that I encourage you to pay attention to is not letting your teen's upping of the ante handcuff you as parents. You need to continue to provide the consistent structure that unemotional parenting teaches. When a teenager behaves in negative or dangerous ways, the implied message they are sending is that they need more limits and more parenting in their lives, not less. Parents who respond to the runaway or to the suicidal teen by providing less structure are just completing a vicious cycle. Since the teenager is really calling for more parenting and getting less, they continually act in negative and dangerous ways. Parents need to pay more attention to the teenager's behaviors, to their demands, complaints, or requests. If their behaviors are telling you that they need more support and more parenting, but they are verbally telling you to back off, you must pay attention to the behaviors. If their behaviors become dangerous or even life-threatening, inventory your support systems and utilize the appropriate systems to get the problems under control. You are not completely on your own.

CHAPTER THIRTEEN

You Have the Tools to Get Started

IN CHAPTER THIRTEEN YOU WILL FIND

- Reviewing the tenets of unemotional parenting
- How to set up appropriate contracts with your kids
- Working extra hard the first 60-90 days
- Selecting three to five behaviors to work on
- Reviewing and refining your work
- One final caution--avoiding over-controlling your child

Now you know all the essential elements behind unemotional parenting. You know that your goal as parents is to raise your children to adulthood. You know that you are the principal tool-giver for your kid, and that you can retain this role well into your child's adolescence. You understand that emotionality in your decision-making sets you up for inconsistency and ineffectiveness. You understand that the more ineffective you are as parents, the harder it is for you to move out of that position and begin behaving more effectively. Most importantly, you know that you are not in control of your teenager's choices. This knowledge can help you treat a teen in more developmentally appropriate ways and talk to him or her more directly.

At this point, you might be wondering how to get started in the unemotional parenting approach. This chapter will offer you suggestions on how to do so. Unemotional parenting is not an approach to be tried and discarded. It is a philosophy, and it needs your effort and your strict adherence to make it work. Do not think that you can try this approach one day and then switch to some other approach the next. Just as it is important for you as parents to understand and predict your child's behavioral choices, it is very important for your kids to come to understand and predict your responses. In doing this, they can evaluate their choices, and understand the consequences that accompany their behaviors. When you lose that consistency in your responses, your kids will lose their ability to make appropriate choices. A trial and error approach to parenting, in which a child could conceivably get many different responses to the same problem behavior, will cause you much more work in the long run than will the unemotional parenting approach outlined in this book. Let's get started setting up this program in your house.

STEP ONE: BECOME FAMILIAR WITH THE TENETS
OF UNEMOTIONAL PARENTING.

Spouses, I encourage you to discuss this philosophy of unemotional parenting with each other. Discuss situations where you have let your emotions control your parenting decisions, and whether or not you were successful in these situations. You must believe that unemotional parenting is a successful and applicable parenting approach. Both parents must understand this philosophy in a similar way. It involves knowing the important things in your children's lives and the particulars of their developmental stages. It also requires that you relinquish responsibility for your children's failures. It involves talking to your kids in reasonable ways and stifling your emotional responses to their choices. You must take charge as the principal role model in their lives, because you have control over many of the things that are important to them. You must also learn how to talk to your kids so they feel empowered to make choices and so that they are able to take personal responsibility for their choices. Finally, this approach involves understanding the change from a role of ultimate authority, to one of coach and advisor that takes place as your teenager approaches adulthood.

STEP TWO: INFORM YOUR KIDS THAT THE WINDS OF CHANGE ARE UPON THEM.

It is important to have a family conference or two to inform your kids that you are going to make some changes in the way you respond to them as parents. Tell them that you believe that you have had too many power struggles with them, and admit that you oftentimes have gotten upset with some of their behaviors. Tell them that you believe you have made poor parenting decisions while upset, but that you will strive now to make your parenting decisions without acting on your emotions. In fact, you will actually not make many of the decisions at all, but rather you will be trying to establish appropriate consequences (both positive and negative) in anticipation of your child's choices. You may want to discuss your parenting relationship with your kids during this conference. If it is true, you may want to admit that you and your spouse have often worked against one another, and that your parenting has suffered because of this. Tell your kids that you are going to strive to support one another in the parenting sphere, and let them know that you are going to be talking to each other a lot more than you have in the past, in an effort to ensure consistency. Tell them that you plan on improving your teamwork to become more effective parents. Reviewing some of the problems that have come up in the past is O.K., but I recommend that you really only review the mistakes you made because you responded more out of emotion than out of fairness. I would advise against bringing up a child's specific problems, and discussing how frustrating it is for you when your kid does such and such. The meeting I am talking about here is meant to inform your kids that you want to improve as parents, and that your parenting may look and feel a little different for them than it has in the past. You may want to tell them that your hope is for them to take charge of their own behavior, and you feel that the best way of teaching them personal responsibility is by holding them accountable for their actions, both in a positive sense and when negative consequences have to be applied. You may want to show them this copy of *It Doesn't Take a Village* and what you learned from it. Offer the book for them to peruse. Remember, this family meeting is designed to inform your kids that you want to improve your parenting, cut down on the struggles that have presented themselves in the past, and place your children in charge of their choices. Tell them some of the things that you are going to be doing differently. Tell them how you are going to go about becoming a more consistent team, and how your communication is going to increase and improve. Now you are ready for Step Three.

STEP THREE: TALK ABOUT ALL OF YOUR KIDS' REQUESTS FOR 60 TO 90 DAYS.

This is a crucial, and very difficult, step to take. This step lets your kids know that you are serious about becoming a parenting team, and it forces you to talk to each other about things that previously you would not have consulted about. For 60 to 90 days, you must make an active and conscientious effort to talk to each other regarding all of your parenting decisions. Your child should see this effort. For 60 to 90 days, when your kid makes a request from you (i.e., "Can I have a piece of pie?" "Can I have $10.00 to go to the mall?" "Can I have the car this weekend?" "Can I go to the concert next week with Joe?" "Can I have my friend spend the night?"), it is your job to say, "That is a parenting decision. I will talk to your mom and we will get back to you." The more mundane the request from your kid, the better the opportunity to show him or her that the two of you are communicating together. You want them to know that their parents are discussing their decisions, and that you are going to back one another. Think about how exaggerated it would be if your son or daughter asked you for a dollar to get some ice cream, and you were to respond, "I don't know. That is a parenting decision. I will talk to your mother and we will get back to you." I am instructing you, however, to do just this for 60 to 90 days.

It is not only important that you respond in this way to requests from your kids; it is equally important that they know that any consequence that they receive for behaviors they have chosen has come from both parents. This is probably more difficult for most parenting teams than the request scenario. When Junior argues with mom about something and calls her a vulgar name, the tendency is for mom to respond with a consequence. This is fine if you have used unemotional parenting, and you have established a consequence for vulgar language prior to this event. Then mom can say, "I wonder why you chose to lose $2.00 for calling me a bitch," and apply the established consequence. If it has not been established, I encourage you not to respond with emotion and apply a consequence on the spot. Instead, inform your kid that a consequence will follow when you are able to discuss this situation with the other parent. Can you see how difficult this type of approach will be? It is bound to be difficult because, when you are in the heat of battle, it is very easy to respond in emotional ways. When you are hurt, you often inadvertently try to hurt back, but if you do this, you will have blown it in a couple of ways. You will have blown the role-modeling part of your job, in which you try to show consistency and emotional control. You want to demonstrate that you are responsible for your behaviors, and that thought goes into your behavioral choices. Your goal is to discourage impulsivity, and when you respond emotionally as a parent you are demonstrating this very trait. You will also have blown it in that you will have not consulted with your parenting partner and made appropriate and fair consequences for the behavior in question. When you respond to your kid's choices with your emotional energy driving your response, you are setting yourself up for poor and inconsistent parenting.

For 60 to 90 days after you have informed your kids that you are going to employ unemotional parenting techniques to their behaviors, I urge you to exaggerate your conversations with each other. I urge you to consult each other on any item that involves parental response, no matter how insignificant. This will show them that you are working to change your style and philosophy regarding parenting. Let them know that you have a plan, and you are not responding to daily events in a random way. Talk to each other, work on finding compromises, and support each other so that you can present yourselves in a unified way. The first 60 to 90 days will require more energy and effort from you than any other time in your parenting, but if you put unemotional parenting strategies to work, they will save you much more work and energy than you put into them. In the first 60 to 90 days, you will be charged with giving your kids the strong message that you are parenting together.

STEP FOUR: PICKING SOME TARGET BEHAVIORS

Now you are ready to put unemotional parenting to work. I encourage you to pick three to five of your kid's behaviors that are giving you trouble. Try to be specific about the behavior (i.e., don't say that you don't like Junior's attitude; identify what behaviors you are seeing that you do not want to see anymore, and don't say that your kid is disrespectful, identify which of his or her behaviors are disrespectful). Be specific and as simple as possible.

Now sit down with each other and discuss these three to five behaviors. Try to identify age-appropriate negative and positive consequences to pair with each of these behaviors. Remember to try to apply a different consequence to each behavior. Don't use the same consequence for every problem behavior. Try hard to identify consequences that are appropriate. A kid who fails at school may forgo an after-school job, or an extra-curricular activity until he or she can start getting good grades. A kid who comes home after curfew may lose time off his curfew, or lose his weekend free time until he can display better compliance with the curfew request. A kid who loses his jacket may have to wear last year's coat or purchase his own new one. These are examples of making the consequence fit the crime. I encourage you to add appropriate positive consequences as well. For example, the kid who brings home good grades and shows everybody that he is responsible for his schoolwork may be allowed a later curfew and more free time, or he may be allowed to take on a part-time job for having proven that he has prioritized school. Similarly, the kid who shows that he or she can get in at curfew or earlier may be rewarded with extended free time for being responsible with this limit. The teen who displays maturity and responsibility in looking after his or her possessions certainly might be rewarded with an expensive starter jacket, or a coveted leather outfit. Positive consequences can have a strong relationship to the positive choices the kid is making.

You may want to engage your child's input in this step, and ask him or her what would be a fair consequence for the behavior displayed. If he or she is able to dialogue with you over the consequences in a reasonable way, then you will have a better chance of the verbal contract working. For many kids, however, this is too much to ask, and the parents must come up with the consequences together. Remember that you should not choose consequences for behaviors when you are upset. This must be done when you are able to think about the poor behavioral choice your child has made in rational and unemotional ways.

Do not think that you will be able to address every little nuisance or idiosyncrasy that arises. Pick between three and five behaviors that are troublesome and that you have a hard time being consistent with, and discuss your response to each behavioral choice until both of you agree on a way that you will proceed. Remember not to make one parent do all of the enforcing. If one parent is largely responsible in this area, this will undercut the team approach you are striving for.

In step four, you are trying to identify appropriate consequences for your child's behavioral choices. Make sure these consequences are enforceable, and make sure that you both agree to carry out the enforcement in the same way.

STEP FIVE: INFORMING YOUR CHILD.

In this step, you must find ways to inform your child of how you will respond in the future to their behaviors. It is ideal to present the consequences reached by unemotional parenting when you are in a non-threatening or non-reacting situation. In other words, do not present your new parenting style to your kids when you are about to punish them or when you are reacting to a negative choice they have made. Earlier in the book we talked about how to communicate with your kids, and, believe me, if you learn more effective ways of communicating, you will save yourself a lot of problems and effort.

For each of the three to five behaviors that you have chosen to begin your unemotional parenting with, tell your kid what consequence will follow if he or she chooses to engage in the behavior in question. Make sure, whenever possible, to include a positive consequence to give them some other incentive (i.e., besides avoiding punishment or the removal of privileges) to modify their behavioral choices. Again, tell them in such a way that they understand that they are in total control of their choices, and that you are letting them know what will follow (both positive and negative), depending on what they choose.

With many kids, it is often effective to predict that they will violate the rules that you have set up, and that they will test your resolve to follow through as you have said you will. In some cases, you may also want to predict that when you follow through with the consequence that they have chosen, they will violate your consequence. This is a common reaction from kids who show no respect for curfew or reporting their whereabouts which they display when parents respond to this behavior by grounding them. You must make it very difficult for them to do this, but you must also look at their reaction as just another non-compliant behavior. Predict that your kid will leave the house after he or she has been grounded, and then inform him or her what consequence will follow. Losing a CD player or a starter jacket, or the use of an automobile for an extended time, may be the correct consequence for a teenager who, when grounded, decides to go out anyway. Remember, predicting your child's behavior is an intervention in itself. No one likes to think that others can tell them how they will respond to something. Spend a little time on this one, because you may save a lot of time if you can practice this in a successful way.

Also, remember some of the equalizers that your kid has up his or her sleeve. They will probably respond initially with something like, "Do what you want, it doesn't really affect me," or "I don't care, take my jacket away." They might also up the ante and begin to act out in more serious ways. The "I don't care" response and upping the ante are your teen's ways of getting you back to your inconsistent parenting by pushing your emotional buttons. In unemotional parenting, when these buttons are pushed, nothing will happen.

STEP SIX: REVIEWING YOUR PROGRESS.

It is important for the parents to review their parenting on a weekly basis. You need to discuss how things are going, and identify any pitfalls that have come up so that you can avoid them in the future.

Again, I feel compelled to advise you to not review your parenting or your youngster's behavior when you are in an emotional state. Do not have your conference when you are frustrated or angry with each other, or with your kid. The weekly review process is designed to establish your roots in the unemotional parenting philosophy. I suggest that you review the week's problems with a **solution-oriented** approach; that is, spend your conferences discussing possible solutions to the week's problems, rather than discussing *ad nauseum* the problems themselves. These times are excellent for discussing behaviors that were not talked about when you initiated your unemotional parenting, but which have since come up. All of you will encounter things that were not originally discussed. Some of these things will be responses your kid has given to your new consistent parenting. Other things will include old behaviors that your kid has chosen that have re-emerged. Remember, in unemotional parenting, you are doing better for yourself if you can identify consequences in advance of your child's behaviors. When you are reviewing, you will no doubt spend some time with the new behaviors that have come up. You can spend this time generating negative and positive consequences for these additional behaviors, and continue the parenting approach that you have started.

Try to identify how it feels to parent in unemotional ways. Do you feel as though you have more control over your own emotions? Do you feel that you have more control over your rules and expectations? Are you getting any better compliance from your kid? Remember, while you are reviewing, that you are in the entry stage of this parenting philosophy, and don't allow yourself to get discouraged. Change is very scary and difficult. I have spoken at length about how your kids will try to get you to return to your old way of responding, but I have not talked much about how you as the parent may resist the change you are trying to implement. It would take another book to discuss the full psychological dynamics of change, and I will not go into this here. If you stay focused on your parenting goals, and you stay consistent with the parenting approach that is outlined in this book, you will gradually overcome any reservations that accompany these changes. You may give up some secondary gains that were attached to your old way of parenting, but you will gain far more than you are giving up in the long run when you adopt this parenting philosophy and the parental responses that this book discusses. No doubt when you are reviewing your progress, you will come across situations in which you have fallen back into your emotional parenting style. Try to identify how that felt, and recall how successful your response was. Identifying these occurrences will help you avoid them in the future. Similarly, identify what it feels like to respond to your kid in unemotional ways. That is what we are striving for: to avoid ugly power struggles, and the problems that accompany parental inconsistency.

Ask you parenting partner for help in areas that are difficult for you. Reviewing your progress as a team will get you to understand the areas in which each of you needs additional work. Remind each other that unemotional parenting is not a trial and error philosophy, because this attitude assumes that you may quit your approach when things get tough. Your kids will be the first to pick up on this ambivalence, and they will inevitably respond in ways that promote your inconsistency. They will behave in ways that will make you question yourself and eventually get them what they want.

It is important that you do not quit on yourself. You will still let emotions slip into your parenting. We are emotional beings, and parenting is an emotionally-laden task. Becoming emotional and responding with your emotions can not be avoided. Your task is to learn from this unavoidable dynamic, and to quit using the negative emotions of anger, frustration, and disappointment in dealing with your child, while at the same time continuing to use your positive emotional energy to relate to your kids. You will experience joy, happiness, and pride as you begin to see the rewards of good parenting and hard work.

When you allow frustration, anger, and disappointment to drive your parental responses, you become less effective as a problem-solver and a teacher. When you do act on these emotions, you need to learn from the experiences that are encountered. I encourage you to develop strategies that work for you. For instance, delaying your parental responses, taking time-outs, discussing the incidents with the less emotional parent, or with a counselor, friend, or other adult family member, can all be effective strategies for avoiding inconsistent and emotional parenting. Letting the less emotional parent take the lion's share of the work on the issue in question, and taking a supporting role yourself, is also an effective way of dealing with your kid and your feelings.

Finally, in your review sessions, you should try to bring your children into the conversation. Review your responses to their positive and negative behaviors with them. As advised in step five, you will want to address any new behaviors that have come up, and give them a clear understanding of the consequences that you will attach to their future choices. Keep in mind your child's stage of development and cognitive-emotional level of functioning. Some parents may enlist their children's input in establishing consequences for their actions other parents may simply inform them of the consequences they have attached to each of their children's behavioral choices.

Soon after you have begun unemotional parenting, do a gut check. Have you regained control over your home? Even though your child may be continuing to choose negative consequences (especially as a way of testing your resolve), is your parenting more consistent? Are those feelings of powerlessness gone, or on their way out? Do you know what has caused them? You felt powerless in the past because you frequently parented by the seat of your pants, and tried at the eleventh hour to come up with effective consequences to your child's bad behaviors. Now you can take pride in the fact that your parental choices have resulted in consistency and respectability. When and if you begin to feel powerless again, I'll bet that you have gotten back into the negative cycle of power struggles that characterized your parent-child relationship before you began unemotional parenting.

Get back to the basics. Stay on top of the things that are important in your kid's life. Stay on top of what they are experiencing developmentally. Take special care in the way that you talk to your youngster, and remove yourself from the cycles of helplessness, adversity, and struggle that accompany emotional parenting.

STEP SEVEN: AVOID OVER-CONTROLLING

I feel compelled to discuss one further caution regarding my parenting philosophy. This type of parenting works so well that many parents literally try to over control their kids. I have outlined numerous examples in this book in which unemotional parenting was effective and useful, but if you try to take away the child's brain and choices by over controlling, you will create a different kind of trouble. Remember, unemotional parenting is about you, not about your kids.

Over controlling a teenager is a mistake that parents frequently make. Parents try to teach their kid every lesson they need to learn, and frequently it is the parents who cause many of the power struggles with their teen that they are trying to avoid. Remember the developmental needs of adolescents, and the conflicts they are struggling with. Remember the striving for independence that characterize this age. Your kids have to be different from you, and frequently they choose a variety of ways to show you that they are different: the music they listen to, the style of clothes they wear, their hair styles and their favorite television shows are all ways that they say, "I am not you."

I suggest to you, as parents, not to sweat the small stuff. Identify what things are really important, and those things that go unidentified, turn over to your adolescent. You know that dangerous behaviors, and behaviors that affect a child's future (i.e., legal problems, drugs and alcohol, sexual promiscuity, educational failure, etc.) require parental responses, but other things do not. Do not panic when your pretty fourteen year old turns her hair purple. It may embarrass you in church, but it is really small potatoes. Do not fight your fifteen year old over how clean or dirty he or she keeps a bedroom. Your teens will learn when they cannot find things that are important to them and how time-saving it is to have things in order. Let your teenager study math with his radio on. He is at least studying. In due time, he will find out that unnecessary noise is simply a distraction. Don't replace one obstacle with another, namely yourself. Let your teenager watch MTV, or listen to that ridiculous heavy metal music. These are small things that let them have control in their lives. Many parents take these small examples and make them bigger problems than they really are. Parents think if their kid is listening to heavy metal that are necessarily doing drugs, and parents whose kids buy the latest rap CD think that this makes their children little gangsters. Oftentimes your kid is listening to these kinds of music as a way of saying they are different from you.

One of my clients is a father who insists that his daughter's messy room is the reason for her flunking out of school. He also insists that the messy room causes the girl to steal her sister's clothes, and to keep the family in constant turmoil. This dad chooses repeatedly to engage his daughter in a huge struggle over keeping her room clean. This struggle, which dad often loses, only serves to confuse the daughter. She experiences her parents as the major source of conflicts in her life, and she has a hard time differentiating between major problem behaviors and peccadilloes like having a messy room. Since her parents fight with her over everything, she equates the struggle about her dirty room with the struggle that occurs when she sneaks out of her room at 3:00 a.m. Both behaviors get similar responses from her dad, and, as a result, she is just as likely to choose to sneak out as she is to leave messes in her room. Please, parents, do not over control your teenager. Allow them to be different from you in some ways. Let them know that you will provide guidance in important matters, but that you will let them handle the small stuff. The young lady who keeps her room looking like a pigpen is not flunking out of school because of it, and her room is certainly not keeping the family in turmoil. Rather, a ridiculous power struggle is occurring because her room does not look the way her dad wants it to, and all sorts of unrelated problems are being tied into this struggle. No wonder the fifteen year old girl does not have a sense of what is truly important as she goes about testing the family rules. Her parents need to hold her accountable for the problems that are arising because she is disorganized and sloppy. They need to make her do her own laundry, and then see how long she continues to throw her clothes on the floor. When she has to wear dirty or wrinkled clothes to school, she will realize the benefit of taking better care of her clothes and her room.

The point here is to keep in mind your child's developmental stages, and to use this knowledge to make things easier in your life, as well as theirs. Don't use unemotional parenting to control the things in your kid's life that really do not need control. It is O.K. to allow your child or teenager to be immature, and to make some immature decisions. If you can't be childish in your childhood, when else can you be? Move away from the "divine right of kings" mentality that declares "This is my house, and you do not need to know my reasons," or "I said so," and move into the coaching mentality, in which you are still in charge of the game plan, but you are enlisting team support to reach your goal. Let your child or teenager be a player on that team.

Make the difficult part of the parenting job easier, and continue to enjoy the pleasurable parts of watching your children grow.

BIBLIOGRAPHY AND REFERENCES

Bibliography

Dr. Benjamin Spock (1946) *Dr. Spock's Baby and Child Care.* Copyright 1945, 1946, 1957, 1968, 1976, 1985 and 1992. Pocket Books Publisher, Simon and Schuster Inc.

Foster Cline M.D. and Jim Fay (1992) *Parenting Teens with Love and Logic.* Publishers Pinon Press.

Jay Haley (1978) *Leaving Home.* Publishers Bantam Books

Phyliss York, David York, and Ted Wachtel (1984) *Tough Love and Tough Love Solutions.* Bantam Books-Double Day Publishers

Gordon Thomas (1970) *Parent Effectiveness Training P.E.T.* Penguin Book Publishers

References

Alcoholics Anonymous 12-Step program for Persons suffering from Alcohol Addiction. Meetings and support services in communities world wide.

Narcotics Anonymous (1987) 5th Edition World Service Office Inc. Publishers Van Nuys California. 12-Step program for persons suffering from Narcotic addiction. Meetings and support services in communities world wide.

Alanon 12-Step Program for persons with family members who are addicted to substances. Meetings and support programs world wide.

Coda 12-Step program for persons who display co-dependency personality traits and behaviors. Meetings and support programs in communities world wide.

Parent Effectiveness Training. See Bibliography above. Courses designed to help parents deal with difficult child rearing situations. Contact your local mental health center for more information.

Tough Love Support Groups. See Bibliography above. Offered in Communities throughout the United States.